August Wilhelm Grube, Levi Seeley

Grube's Method of Teaching Arithmetic

Explained and Illustrated, also the Improvements upon the Method....

August Wilhelm Grube, Levi Seeley

Grube's Method of Teaching Arithmetic
Explained and Illustrated, also the Improvements upon the Method....

ISBN/EAN: 9783337165482

Printed in Europe, USA, Canada, Australia, Japan

Cover: Foto ©Paul-Georg Meister /pixelio.de

More available books at **www.hansebooks.com**

GRUBÉ'S

METHOD OF TEACHING

ARITHMETIC.

Explained and Illustrated. Also the improvements upon the method made by the followers of Grubé in Germany.

BY

LEVI SEELEY, A.M., PH.D. (*Leipsic*).

"THAT MAN WILL BE A BENEFACTOR OF HIS RACE WHO SHALL TEACH US HOW TO MANAGE RIGHTLY THE FIRST YEARS OF A CHILD'S EDUCATION."
Garfield.

NEW YORK AND CHICAGO:

E. L. KELLOGG & CO.

1891.

PREFACE.

THERE is a widespread feeling among American teachers that there is need of better methods of teaching Number, especially in the primary classes. During the last few years, the Grube System, having been introduced into a few schools and discussed at teachers' institutes and in educational journals, has attracted the attention of thoughtful educators in various parts of our land. Many of the later Arithmetics have devoted a few pages in outlining this system or in giving a few hints in regard to it. The excellent results apparent in those schools that have tried the system, the enthusiasm of its adherents, and the belief that it is based on sound philosophical principles, have created a desire to a better understanding of it. The design of this little book is to give a plain, concise exposition of the Grube theory, and, at the same time, to illustrate the method of teaching Number in accordance with it. It is intended to be a helpful book for the primary teacher.

This book is not simply a translation of Grube's treatise, nor is it the Grube system exclusively; it includes *all of that system, and in addition the latest and best ideas of the disciples of Grube in Germany,* whose works were studied and whose personal acquaintance was made by the author in their school-rooms and in their educational associations during a three years' study of the German schools.

In the preparation of this book I have examined with care the following works : Grube's "Leitfaden für das Rechnen in der Elementarschule" (the original exposition of Grube's system), German works on Arithmetic by Bräutigam, Göpfert, Lincke, Schellen, Berthelt und Petermann, Rein's "Theorie und Praxis," Soldan's "Grube's Method," Indianapolis School Manual of 1876, Quincy (Mass.) Course of Study of 1879, and other treatises.

LEVI SEELEY.

LAKE FOREST, ILL., 1888.

SKETCH OF GRUBE.

AUGUST WILHELM GRUBE was born in Wernigerode at the foot of the Harz Mountains, Germany, on the 16th of December, 1816. His father was a tailor, and August was his only child. He commenced school when four years of age, and very early decided to devote himself to teaching. Grube often said in later years that it was his love for his teacher that awakened in him the wish to become a teacher.

When eight years of age he entered the Lyceum of his native city, where he remained till his fifteenth year, after which he entered the Teachers' Seminary at Weissenfels near Leipzig. In 1836, when twenty years of age, he completed his work here, and obtained a testimonial which stated that Grube was well fitted to teach in the best grade of schools. After teaching a short time in a public school, he took the position of family teacher (Hauslehrer) in the family of a count in the province of Posen. A like position in the family of a wealthy manufacturer near Bregenz occupied his time until he gave up teaching and devoted himself to authorship. He died January 27, 1884.

"Grube was one of the most fruitful and, at the same time, most important pedagogical authors of the present time; a man endowed with philosophical penetration and sound knowledge, great from inclination and character, likewise rich in the experiences of life and of the schoolroom. He has by means of his writings exercised an extensive, blessed influence upon the educators of our time."

His works cover all departments of pedagogics. From the many we name "Pedagogical Studies and Criticisms" (Pädagogische Studien und Kritiken), in one part of which he discusses "Darwinism and its Consequences," taking a stand against Darwin. Especially has Grube rendered great service to the young by his "Geographical Character-pictures" (Geographischen Charakterbilder), "Biographies from Natural Science" (Biographien aus der Naturkunde), "Character-pictures from History and Tradition" (Charakterbilder aus der Geschichte und Sage). Grube was the forerunner of new methods of teaching geography in Germany. He opposed the practice of making the study of geography a memorizing of numbers and facts, and arranged the material to be taught so that it could be used to advantage. He connected the teaching of geography with pictures of the landscape, with productions, temperature of the country, and would show how the customs, religion, government, history, and happiness of the people are related to and dependent upon the country.

But of particular interest to us in connection with this work is Grube's "Guide for Reckoning in the Elementary School, according to the Principles of an Inventive Method" (Leitfaden für das Rechnen in der Elementarschule, nach den Grundsätzen einer heuristischen Methode). This book marked an epoch in the teaching of Number in Germany and has exerted a wide influence on American teaching.

CONTENTS.

INTRODUCTION.

PESTALOZZI was the pioneer who broke new ground in elementary instruction and led the way from mechanical, abstract methods to those which are more natural and psychological. He laid down the principle *that all mathematical-knowledge is founded upon immediate observation, and therefore must proceed from the concrete to the general or abstract by means of innumerable examples.* This discovery was not only of vast importance to pupils in the schools, but it opened up to teachers the psychological principles of all pedagogics.

In 1842, only fifteen years after Pestalozzi's death, appeared Grube's "Leitfaden für das Rechnen in der Elementarschule." In this work Grube gives a thoroughly developed system of teaching number. Pestalozzi was unfortunately lacking in system. While he brought to light pedagogical principles, he developed no system of pedagogics. He taught the world that the proper way to teach the child is to go directly to Nature, let her operate on the mind and follow her harmonious development. Grube found the germ of his system in Pestalozzi's teachings, but went farther than his master in that he broke away from the idea of teaching the four processes, addition, subtraction, multiplication, and division, separately and in the order named. This is one of the great and most important features of the Grube system. Grube held that the four simple processes of arithmetic should go together in the small numbers, believing it to be the natural process of the mind.

By the use of objects the child is brought to see the relations of numbers until he is able to reproduce the relations without the objects. As the elementary work properly covers the period from the sixth to the tenth year, the period of observation, and as the method is purely elementary, Grube discusses only the first four years' work. His plan provides for three hours (full hours) per week. The end to be reached is a thorough knowledge of the fundamental rules and common fractions. His work is divided into three parts or courses:

I. Whole numbers from 1 to 100, employing the first two years.

II. Whole numbers above 100, employing the third school year.

III. Fractions, employing the fourth year.

He lays down the work definitely for each half-year, which we shall fully discuss later.

ADVANTAGES OF GRUBE'S METHOD.

I. It recognizes the psychological fact that nearly all the knowledge obtained by the child in its earlier years is by means of the senses.

By observation and not by reasoning does the child gain his first knowledge of number. In the earlier years the child's reasoning powers must be brought very little into play. He is not yet especially ready for reasoning, and Nature did not intend that he shall gain knowledge at this early period through the reason. He is eager for knowledge, but such knowledge as is obtainable by the senses. He learns mechanically. He comes to know all the combinations and manipulations taught him so as to give them with absolute accuracy and great rapidity without stopping to think.

II. As it makes the first year's work a study of the numbers 1 to 10 it lays a solid foundation.

The knowledge thus obtained becomes an acquirement which will be a methodical, substantial product. According to our usual crude methods this may seem but little work for an entire year, yet by this scientific study the first ten numbers will be found to furnish ample work. They are the foundation of the whole number system ; all larger numbers are only a repetition, in a sense, of the first orders. The more thoroughly the numbers from one to ten are known, the surer and more rapid will be all later work in arithmetic. Let this foundation be well laid and the structure is well begun. Within these limits there is so much rich material for all-sided practical applications that the teacher will find plenty to do to accomplish the teaching of the first ten numbers in one year.

III. The Grube method progresses gradually and naturally according to the ability of the child.

It proceeds from the knowledge already gained to new knowledge by a very easy step. The knowledge possessed is utilized in mastering new knowledge. The child must not be subjected to mental over-exertion at any period. This is especially dangerous during the first years. The Grube method does not require too much, and yet it gives endless and suitable variety so that the child does not tire of number.

IV. It develops the mental powers evenly and in all directions.

One-sided teaching should always be avoided. All development should be harmonious and natural. Grube considers each number by itself as an entirety and teaches all about it completely, thus building the mathematical structure step by step.

V. Elementary teaching of number should proceed from observation, or, better, it should proceed from things.

Grube's system calls for the use of things—balls, marbles, cubes, blocks. It uses objects repeatedly until the child is thorough master of the number and can make the combinations abstractly. After a time the simple remembrance of the objects used will always be sufficient to recall to the consciousness the number until no object is longer necessary and the pure relations of numbers are fixed. Then the child needs no object, or intermediate process, to help him to know the number, but he knows it instantly, and the simple, fundamental processes are mechanical. So we pass from the object to the symbol, from this to the comprehension of number, and lead in this way the interest from the empire of objects over to the empire of the number forms.

VI. The Grube method makes the teaching of number an excellent language-lesson.

The answers and statements are to be complete sentences; and as the subject is always kept within the ability of the child to comprehend, the number-lesson becomes one of the most valuable means of teaching language.

VII. The child acquires the habit of close observation.

As only that which is within the child's comprehension is brought before him, and as familiar objects are placed before him so frequently and so systematically, he acquires the habit of accurate and close observation. He learns to *see* what is brought to his notice, and to see all about it. This is one of the most important features of the Grube method, in that it is thoroughly psychological.

VIII. It develops and trains the attention.

As the child can understand the matter, it interests him, and interest is the first factor of attention. Because of its harmonious, all-sided development it cultivates the power of attention and leads the child to the habit of commanding and fixing the attention at will.

IX. It forms the habit of thoroughness in the child.

Mastering each number in all its details and possible combinations, it becomes, like a habit, a part of the very being of the child, until he is able to use it exactly as he uses the eye or the hand, without conscious thought.

Beginning thus early in his school life to gain a thorough mastery of each step, he is led to desire mastery in other departments of learning and of practical life.

X. The Grube method gives pleasure and awakens a love for the study of number.

If the pleasure of work is not found in the work itself, all incentives and threatenings will be in vain. The desire to know a thing must be produced in the child himself. The impulse can begin in the young mind only when there is the consciousness of continual unity in the development of his powers, and then he will be driven by this impulse to further development by his self-activity. This method contains such unity and thus awakens in the child a love for the subject.

XI. It makes the child self-active in a proper manner.

Becoming complete master of a number, he is able to combine and operate with it by making original examples. Thus number becomes to him from the first a living, practical reality.

XII. The Grube method is a logical one.

It proceeds systematically and according to an order of sequence; it is psychological in that it teaches the use of the senses, in that it proceeds from the simple to the more difficult, and in that it goes out from the known to unknown and makes constant use of the known; it is practical because it gives a sure foundation for all future work in arithmetic, and because it brings the child immediately to measure and compare numbers and to make use of the relations of the same.

DIRECTIONS TO TEACHERS.

THE first course includes whole numbers 1 to 100. Two years are required for this work, the first year being spent on 1 to 10 and the second on the rest, 10 to 100.

It must not be forgotten that the number-lesson must at the same time be a language-lesson. It is of the highest importance that the child give his answers in complete sentences, plainly spoken, with clear accent. Great importance must be attached to the explanation of every example from the outset. So long as the child is not master of the language necessary to express the operations performed with the number, he is not master of the representation or idea of the number itself, he does not know the number.

An example is not finished when the answer is found, but when it has been analyzed. The language may be taken as a safe test that a pupil has completely mastered a step.

So far as possible the pupil must be led to speak for himself and not to depend upon half the answer being put into his mouth by the teacher. Concert and individual answers must interchange in order that the interest of the class be maintained.

The uniform objects to be used are the fingers and blocks; for blackboard or slate use simple straight lines. Too many kinds of objects must not be used. The child has only a certain amount of strength and mental power which he can apply, and his interest must not be divided.

The mental comprehension of number is disturbed if things which awaken other ideas or desires are employed. The mind is capable of only a certain amount of interest, and when this interest is wholly or partly withdrawn but little can be expected for the particular thing at hand.

For this reason, while teaching the abstract number, there should be but few things shown the child, and these should be simple and uniformly the same. The best things are blocks, which awaken little interest in themselves, and these must be the chief objects used throughout. Other objects should be referred to after the child has a number well fixed, by way of application, but should seldom be shown him, at least during the study of the first numbers. Thus apples, nuts, etc., which awaken desire, stimulate the appetite, and thus divide the attention, must not be used as objects in teaching number. All the interest which the child gives to the color, taste, etc., of objects is just so much lost to number..

The operations in any step consist simply of comparing and measuring what has been gained in the preceding steps with that which is new. The child proceeds from the known to the unknown, from the easy to the difficult; hence the method must follow a psychological law. The *pure* number is first learned, and then it is applied to *things* in order to fix it and make its practical use apparent.

The work of teaching a number is not complete until the child has been taught to make neatly and with dispatch the figure which stands for the number. This makes excellent employment for the children at their seats, and is a good preparation for written arithmetic, for which the foundation is being laid.

Go slowly—do not measure the ability of the child by your ability; bring yourself down to the level of the child's mind; be patient; repeat everything many times; review daily; use many examples and lead the children to make original problems.

Lastly, do not expect too much of the children; give them the kind and quantity of food that they can digest, remembering that real, sound, intellectual growth is slow, especially at the beginning.

THE FIRST YEAR: 1-10.

THE work of the first year embraces a study of the numbers, 1, 2, 3, 4, 5, 6, 7, 8, 9, 10. Each number is taken by itself, measured by those that precede it, compared and studied in all its possible operations.

FIRST STEP.

THE ONE.*

The one can only be measured by itself. The child has only to learn the idea of unity.

---

* Many insist that the child already knows the *one*, and that it is folly to spend time in teaching it. But it must not be forgotten that the child when he enters school must begin the study of number, must begin to form habits of correct speaking and thinking, must learn to observe carefully what is done, to tell what he sees done, and to answer in complete sentences. Then, too, the Grube system builds step by step, always making use of the knowledge possessed. The *one* is the first step. For these reasons and for these purposes a short time can be profitably spent with the *one*. It may be further added that the fact of the child's knowing the *one* will make it especially valuable in getting him to feel confidence in himself, an important matter for the child when he begins school.

I. The Pure (Abstract) Number.*

(*The teacher shows the block.*) How many have I ?
P. You have *one.*
T. Charles, take this block.   Now how many has Charles ?
P. Charles has *one.*
T. Charles, give it to me.   Now how many has Charles ?
P. Charles has *none.*
T. How many have I ?
P. You have one.

(Lead the children to watch the movements of the teacher, to describe accurately what he does.

Many other questions similar to the above can be given.   Great care must be given to the language.   Cor-

---

* The idea of a number is given the child by the use of an object or objects which are placed before him to see.   He sees the concrete form, but does not name it.   It suggests to him the abstract number.   Thus when the child sees one block he is led to think of it as a *one*, two blocks as a *two*, three blocks as a *three*, etc.   Do not let the child say "one block," "two blocks," but simply "one," "two," etc.   Requiring the child to name the object withdraws his attention from the number itself.   It is much easier for him to speak of the abstract number, and it is also easier for him to read and write it.   The block gives him the picture of the number, and that is all that is wanted of it ; after getting the picture of it he only needs to use the name that stands for the number.   After becoming thoroughly familiar with the number, the child must go a step farther and use it with various objects and make application of it.   This procedure is entirely psychological in that it proceeds from the simple to the complex, from the known to the unknown.

rect statements must be given. *Never accept anything else.*)

T. Now let us put this *one* on the board (*makes a drawing of the block*). How many have I?

P. You have one.

T. But it takes too long to make this kind of a one; we will let this I stand for our one. How many have I?

P. You have I.

(The use of the mark is simply to save time. The child readily proceeds from the object [the block] to its picture, and from that to the straight mark [I] as standing for one.)

T. Now we will learn to make something else that stands for one. Watch me and see what it is. It is this *1*. What does that stand for?

P. That stands for one.

T. Now you may make that on your slates.

(By this method the pupils are taught the figure. The block, its picture, and the mark [I] must be taught as the number *one*. The child thinks of them only as the *one*. But he must learn to make the character which stands for the one; namely, the figure [*1*]. No number must be left and no step be considered complete until the pupils have learned to make the figure which stands for the number. Great care must be taken by the teacher not to confuse the *number* with the *figure*.)

II. The Applied Number.

T. What thing do you find but once in the school-room?

P. I find *one* stove (desk, clock, etc.).

T. What have you *one* of at home?

P. I have one dog (cat, sled, etc.).

(But little time need be given to the one, the aim being chiefly to get good expressions from the children, and to start them in the mode of thought to be pursued hereafter with the other numbers.)

SECOND STEP.

THE TWO.

I. The Pure Number.—*Measuring and Comparing.*

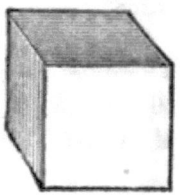 

T. How many have I ?

P. You have *two.*

T. (*Takes a block in each hand and holds up one.*) What have I here ?

P. You have *one.*

T. And what have I here ? (*the other hand.*)

P. You have also *one.*

T. Now watch and see what I do. (*Moves the hands holding the blocks slowly together.*) What did I do?

P. You put one and one together.

(Continue this operation until they can make a good statement of the fact.)

T. Very well.   Now we will put this little story on the board.   ☐ and ☐ make ☐ ☐.   That is good ; but I can make these marks [I I] instead of the pictures [☐ ☐], and that will be easier.   What have I here [I I]?

P. You have two.

T. But I can make something else which means two. It is this : *2.*   What have I now?

P. You have two.

(The teacher should in this manner teach each figure. When the pupils have learned the number, and have seen it expressed by pictures of blocks and by marks, they are then ready to learn the simplest way of expressing it, that is, by the figure.   Make the figure slowly before the class, so that they can imitate your manner of making it.)

T. Now what have I ?   (Two blocks shown together.)

P. You have a *two*.

(It is most important here that the child be taught that the two cubes is a 2 and not two blocks.   The child must think of it in its entirety—a two.)

T. How many 2's have I ?

P. You have one 2.

T. How many times have I 2 ?

P. You have 2 one time or once.

T. How many does one 2 make ?

P. One 2 makes 2.

T. Now let me write—One 2 is 2.

(This will be reached only after repeated and patient efforts, but it pays to give the necessary time, because it is fundamental and all later work will be better and more easily done.   Show the blocks and lead the child to see for himself.   Always go back to the blocks when the child is in doubt.   After the child has learned the figure it may be used to indicate the number.   Until then use objects, pictures, or marks to stand for the number.)

T. Again, notice what I have.   (*The two blocks in one hand.*)

P. You have 2.

T. Now see what I do.   (*The teacher slowly takes* 1 *from* 2.)

P. You took 1 away from 2.

T. And what does that leave ?

P. It leaves 1.

T. Who will tell me the whole story about what I did ?

P. You took 1 away from 2 and it left 1.

T. Good ; we will write that also.

☐☐ less ☐ leaves ☐.

Very well ; now we will write that another way.

2 less 1 leaves 1.

Let us now see what else we can do.   (*The teacher holds the* 2 *blocks before the children and takes* 1 *away.*)   What have I done ?

P. You have taken 1 away.

(*Teacher then takes the other away.*)   Now what have I done ?

P. You have taken 1 away again.
T. How many times have I taken 1 away from 2?
P. You have taken 1 away two times.
T. Then how many 1's are there in 2?
P. There are two 1's in 2.
T. Now we will write that on the board.

In 2 there are two 1's.

Or we may say 2 divided by 1 makes 2.

(This last statement will be somewhat difficult for the child, and should not be attempted until by the method above given he has mastered the idea. Then we may teach this as another way of expressing the same thing. It is necessary that the child learn this way of expressing division, as it is the simplest expression and is the form that he will most often meet with. After mastering the idea it will not take long for the child to learn the form in common use.)

T. Now we will write what we have learned about 2.

1 and 1 make 2.

One 2 is a 2 or makes a 2.

Two 1's are a 2 or make a 2.

2 less 1 is 1.

In a 2 there are two 1's.*

In a 2 there is one 2.

(At this time the signs can be taught. Write each expression using the words, and underneath write the same expression using the signs.) For example:

1 and 1 make 2,

$1 + 1 = 2.$

2 divided by 1 makes 2.

$2 \div 1 = 2.$

(Require the child to read the expression containing the words, and then that containing the signs. He must read both exactly alike. Hereafter use only signs, and require the pupils to make and use them. Go slowly, repeat many times, seek to get correct expressions, teach the

---

* I can take 1 from 2 twice.

children to observe accurately what you do and to describe it.)

The four processes must be repeated until the pupils can give all operations with great rapidity. They must also be able to make their statements fluently, to read readily from the board, and to write exercises from dictation, all to be included within the 2.

The pupil must be able to answer such combinations as follows, the teacher developing them by use of the blocks :

What number is found twice in 2 ?

Of what number is 2 the double ?

Of what number is 1 the half ?

What number must I double in order to get 2 ?

I know a number which has 1 more than 1. What is it ?

What number must I add to 1 in order to get 2 ?

All possible combinations of the 2 should thus be given.

II. The Applied Number.

(The pupils are now prepared to apply their knowledge in practical examples embracing other objects than the blocks. It is no longer necessary to show them the objects. Let them also make examples.)

Fred had 2 cents and spent 1 cent for cherries. How much had he left ?

A slate pencil cost one cent. How much will 2 pencils cost ?

Charles had 1 dime in his savings bank ; his sister had twice as many. How many had his sister ?

If a cake cost 1 cent, how many cakes can you buy for 2 cents ?

James had 2 apples and Frank had half as many. How many had Frank ?

George had 1 marble and John twice as many. How many had John ?

THIRD STEP.

THE THREE.

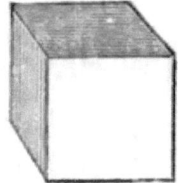

I. The Pure Number.—*Measuring and Comparing.*
(a)—With one.

(The cubes should be placed on a table where all the class can see what is done with them. It is inconvenient to operate with three or more blocks in the hands. Therefore, the blocks must be shown on the table.)

T. How many have I ?   (*Shows the 3 blocks separately.*)
P. You have 1 + 1 + 1.
T. How many is that?
P. 1 + 1 + 1 = | | |.
T. Good ; I will print this little story on the board :

$$\square + \square + \square = \square\ \square\ \square,$$

then

$$1 + 1 + 1 = |\ |\ |.$$

(When sure that the pupils know the 3, he writes 1 + 1 + 1 = 3, teaching the figure 3 by the same method as the 2 was taught. The symbol representing the number must be taught as soon as the pupils have obtained the idea of the number, and not before. After they have learned the figure which stands for a number, no other characters need be used to represent the number.)

T. Now tell me how many times I have 1. (*Picks up the blocks one after another, the children counting.*)
P. You have one 3 times.

T. One 3 times makes how many?
P. One 3 times makes 3.
T. Then how many are 3 times one?
P. 3 times 1 are 3, or

$$3 \times 1 = 3.$$

T. Now, what have I done? (*Holds up the 3 blocks and takes 1 away.*)
P. You have taken 1 away from 3.
T. How many are left?
P. There are 2 left.
T. Who will write that for me on the board?
P. (*Child writes* $3 - 1 = 2$.)
T. What else have I done? (*Takes another block away from the remaining 2.*)
P. You have taken 1 away from the 2.
T. How many does that leave?
P. It leaves 1.
T. Now read $3 - 1 - 1 = 1$.
Still, again, how many times can I take 1 away from 3? (*Takes 1 away 3 times, children counting.*)
P. You can take 1 away 3 times.
T. Then how many ones are there in 3?
P. There are 3 ones in 3.
T. Then I will write 1 in $3 = 3$ or $3 \div 1 = 3$. Now see what we have learned.

$$
\begin{array}{l}
1 \\ 1 \\ 1 \\ 1
\end{array}
\left\{
\begin{array}{l}
1 + 1 + 1 = 3 \\
3 \times 1 \quad\;\; = 3 \\
3 - 1 - 1 = 1 \\
3 \div 1 \quad\;\; = 3
\end{array}
\right.
$$

(b)—*Measuring with* 2.

(In the same manner the following tables will be developed, the children always seeing the manipulations with the blocks and acquiring the statements of themselves. If a child hesitates and does not yet comprehend, go over the operations again. Call him up and let him handle the blocks until he has mastered the process and understands the relations.)

$$\text{I I}\ \begin{cases} 2 + 1 = 3,\ 1 + 2 = 3 \\ 1 \times 2 + 1 \qquad\quad = 3 \\ 3 - 2 = 1,\ 3 - 1 = 2 \\ 3 \div 2 = 1,\ \text{and I remainder.*} \end{cases}$$

3 is 1 more than what?
3 is 1 more than 2.
3 is 2 more than what?
3 is 2 more than 1.
2 is 1 less than what?
2 is 1 less than 3.
In the same manner find that—
1 is 2 less than 3.
3 is 3 × 1.
1 is $\frac{1}{3}$ of 3.†
What 3 equal numbers make 3?
What numbers with 1 make 3?
The 3 contains a 2 and a 1.

(All of these combinations have been wrought out using the blocks. Use only the blocks, the fingers and marks. Do not divide the attention by the introduction of new objects or things that awaken a desire of possession in

---

* This should be developed as follows :
T. How many have I here ? (*Holding up the* 3 *blocks.*)
P. You have 3.
T. How many ones in it ?
P. There are 3 ones.
T. Now see how many twos you can find. (*Children take the blocks and find out for themselves.*) How many are there ?
P. There is one 2.
T. Who will find another 2 ?
P. There is no other 2, there is only 1 left.
T. Then how many twos in 3 ?
P. There is one 2.
T. And what is there left ?
P. There is 1 left.
T. Now tell me the whole story.
P. In 3 there is one 2 and 1 left.
T. Very well, but I like the word *remainder* instead of *left.* Now try again.
P. In 3 there is one 2 and 1 remainder.
† To teach this I would take 3 blocks and place 1 block near them. Then ask which is the larger and how many times. Reverse the process, and ask which is the smaller, how many of the ones it takes to make a three, and finally, what part of the three the one is.

the child. Require the pupils to make the figures 1, 2, 3 forwards and backwards, thus, 1, 2, 3, 3, 2, 1.)

Rapid Work.

Teacher gives examples orally as rapidly as possible, the children giving only the answer.

How many are $3 - 1 - 1 + 1$?

$3 \times 1 - 2 \times 1 - 1 = ?$

$1 + 1 \times 1 + 1 - 3 = ?$

$3 - 2 + 1 + 1 - 2 = ?$

$2 + 1 + 1 - 2 + 1 - 1 = ?$

(Many examples of this kind should be given until the pupils are able to give the answer instantly. This is largely oral work.)

Combining.

From what number can you take the double of 1 and still have 1 remaining?

What number is 3 times 1?

I use a number once, and then once again, and then once again, and obtain 3. What is the number?

II. The Applied Number.

If you would buy a 3-cent stamp, how many cents must you have?

Anna had a 3-cent piece, and bought 2 cents' worth of candy. How much change should she get?

If a pencil cost 1 cent, how much will 3 pencils cost?

Charles has 2 apples and 1 apple. How many apples has he?

Mary divided 3 flowers among her father, mother, and brother. How did she divide them?

Martha, Fanny, and William have each 1 book. How many books have they?

A boy had 3 apples and ate 1 apple. How many had he left?

David has 1 dollar. How much more must he earn in order to have 3 dollars?

An uncle divided 3 dimes equally among his 3 nieces. How much did each receive?

My father gave each of his boys 1 dollar, and it took 3 dollars. How many boys had he?

FOURTH STEP.

THE FOUR.

 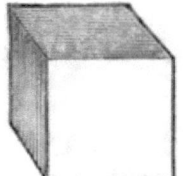 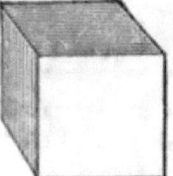 

(It will not be necessary longer to pursue the question and answer method, as it has been sufficiently illustrated. The course indicated should be pursued for all subsequent numbers. Develop all the relations which come under "Measuring and Comparing" by use of the blocks. Lead the children to the statement of what you develop. The further you proceed the greater opportunity for variety, but limit that to such as may be obtained by use of such objects as have been heretofore specified, namely, blocks, fingers, marks.)

I. The Pure Number.—*Measuring and Comparing.*

(*a*) With 1.

$$
\begin{array}{ll}
\text{I I I I} & 4 \\
\begin{array}{l} \text{I } 1 \\ \text{I } 1 \\ \text{I } 1 \\ \text{I } 1 \end{array}
\left\{
\begin{array}{l}
1 + 1 + 1 + 1 = 4,\ 1 + 1 = 2 + 2 = 4. \\
4 \times 1 = 4. \\
4 - 1 - 1 - 1 = 1. \\
4 \div 1 = 4.
\end{array}
\right.
\end{array}
$$

(*b*) With 2.

$$
\begin{array}{l}
\text{I I 2} \\ \text{I I 2}
\end{array}
\left\{
\begin{array}{l}
2 + 2 = 4. \\
2 \times 2 = 4. \\
4 - 2 = 2. \\
4 \div 2 = 2.
\end{array}
\right.
$$

(*c*) With 3.

$$3 + 1 = 4, \ 1 + 3 = 4.$$
$$1 \times 3 + 1 = 4.$$
$$4 - 3 = 1, \ 4 - 1 = 3.$$
$4 \div 3 = 1$ and 1 remainder (3 in 4 once, and 1 remainder.)

How many more legs has a horse than a man?

How many times the number of wheels of a bicycle has a wagon?

How many more legs has a chair than a piano-stool?

4 is how many more than 3?

(Bring out the following facts with the blocks):

4 is 1 more than 3, 2 more than 2, 3 more than 1.

3 is 1 less than 4, 1 more than 2, 2 more than 1.

2 is 2 less than 4, 1 less than 3, 1 more than 1.

1 is 3 less than 4, 2 less than 3, 1 less than 2.

4 is 4 times 1, 2 times (or double) 2.

1 is one fourth of 4, 2 is one half of 4.

Of what equal and what unequal numbers is 4 made up?

*Rapid Work.**

$2 \times 2 - 3 + 2 \times 1 + 1 - 2$ doubled $= ?$

$4 - 1 - 1 - 1 + 1 - 3$ is how much less than 4?

$3 - 1 \times 2 - 3 + 2 + 1 \div 2 = ?$

$2 \times 2 \times 1 - 3 + 2 - 1 \times 2 \div 3 = ?$

$1 + 1 + 1 - 2 \times 4 - 3 \times 2 = ?$

$4 \div 2 + 1 + 1 - 3 - 1 = ?$

(Continue the work as described before, always keeping within the combinations of the 4.)

Combining.

What number must I take 2 times in order to get 4?

Of what number is 4 the double?

---

* These expressions are intended only for dictation, the pupil working as fast as they are dictated, and obtaining the result of each step with no reference to what is to follow. Thus $3 - 1 \times 2 - 3 + 2 + 1 + 2$ would be when worked out from dictation $3 - 1 = 2$, $2 \times 2 = 4$, $4 - 3 = 1$, $1 + 2 = 3$, $3 + 1 = 4$, $4 \div 2 = 2$. Of course the pupils do not repeat the numbers as in the exercises here given, but obtain each result mentally as soon as the teacher dictates. The end sought is *rapidity* as well as accuracy. When expressions are written for the pupils,

Of what number is 2 the half?
Of what number is 1 the fourth?
What number can be taken twice away from 4?
What number is 3 greater than 1?
How much must I add to the half of 4 in order to get 4?
How many times 1 is the half of 4 less than 3?
If I take 1 from 4, how many times 1 have I left?
If I add 1 to 1, what part of 4 have I?
If I take 3 from 4, what part of 3 have I left?
How much is the half of 4 more than the third of 3?
How much is the fourth of 4 less than the half of 4?

II. The Applied Number.

Caroline had 4 tulips in her vase which she neglected to water. One wilted, then another, then another. How many had she left?

How many cents in 2 two-cent pieces?

In a one-cent and a three-cent piece?

How many cakes can you buy for 4 cents if each costs 1 cent?

When each costs 2 cents?

If a top costs 2 cents, how much will 2 tops cost?

John paid for 2 cakes a three-cent and a one-cent piece. What was the cost of each?

One quart has 2 pints. How many pints in 2 quarts?

Charles had 4 chestnuts, and gave Frank 1 and Henry 1. How many had he left?

William had 3 peaches and ate 2. How many had he left?

Anna received an orange on Monday, one on Tuesday, one on Wednesday, and one on Thursday. How many did she receive in all?

---

care must be taken to have them mathematically correct and not to include combinations beyond the 4, or the number which is being taught. The above expressions, as well as those which follow later under the head of "Rapid Work," may not always be correct when taken as a whole and considered as a mathematical expression; but they are correct as dictation exercises, and a few are given for the purpose of suggesting the method to the teacher. Such exercises will be found very valuable.

George had 4 apples and ate 1 each day. How many days did they last?

If a pint of milk costs 2 cents, how many pints will 4 cents buy?

What part of 4 cents is 1 cent?

What part of 4 cents is 2 cents?

What part of 1 quart is 1 pint?

What part of 1 gallon is 1 quart?

My father had 3 cows and bought 1 more. How many has he now?

If he sells 2 cows how many will he have left?

Mary had 1 pin and found 3 more. How many had she then?

If a letter requires 2 two-cent stamps, what will it cost to mail it?

I had 4 quarts of milk, and sold 3 quarts. How many quarts had I left?

A mother has 2 sons and 2 daughters. How many children has she?

I have 4 pears which I wish to divide equally between my 2 sisters. How many can I give each?

(Give many examples from the life of the children until they can make application of all the relations contained within the 4. Let them also make examples. Do not let them leave a number for a new step until they can make the figure, perform rapidly all the combinations whether given to them orally, or written on the board, make complete statements of such combinations, and apply them in their own surroundings. The great success of this method depends upon thoroughness in these particulars.)

FIFTH STEP.

THE FIVE.

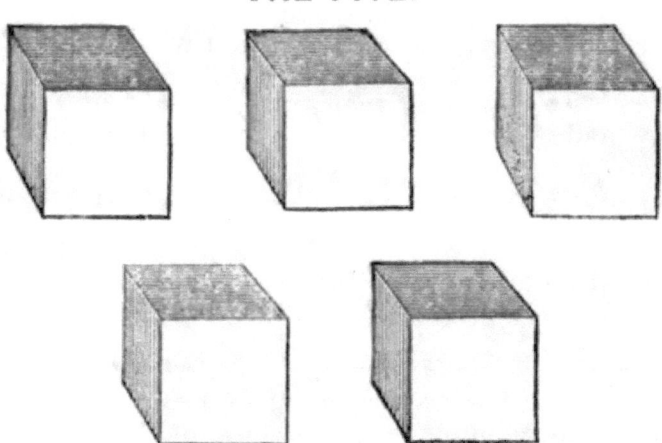

(As it is difficult to work with five blocks in the hands, they should be manipulated on a table before the children so that they can be plainly seen. It would be better still if the children could be gathered around a large table and each have the same number of blocks, so as to perform the same work as the teacher does with hers. The blocks can very well be dropped and only the fingers used after this.)

I. The Pure Number.—*Measuring.*

(*a*) With 1.

$$
\begin{aligned}
&1 + 1 + 1 + 1 + 1 = 5 \\
&5 \times 1 = 5, \ 1 \times 5 = 5 \\
&5 - 1 - 1 - 1 - 1 = 1 \\
&5 \div 1 = 5
\end{aligned}
$$

(*b*) With 2.

$$
\begin{matrix}
\circ\ \circ & 2 \\
\circ\ \circ & 2 \\
\circ & 1
\end{matrix}
\quad
\left\{
\begin{aligned}
&2 + 2 + 1 = 5 \\
&2 \times 2 + 1 = 5 \\
&5 - 2 - 2 = 1 \\
&5 \div 2 = 2\ (1)
\end{aligned}
\right.
$$

(*c*) With 3.

$$
\begin{matrix}
\circ\ \circ\ \circ & 3 \\
\circ\ \circ & 2
\end{matrix}
\quad
\left\{
\begin{aligned}
&3 + 2 = 5,\ 2 + 3 = 5 \\
&1 \times 3 + 2 = 5 \\
&5 - 3 = 2,\ 5 - 2 = 3 \\
&5 \div 3 = 1\ (2)
\end{aligned}
\right.
$$

(*d*) With 4.

$$
\begin{matrix}
\circ\ \circ\ \circ\ \circ & 4 \\
\circ & 1
\end{matrix}
\quad
\left\{
\begin{aligned}
&4 + 1 = 5,\ 1 + 4 = 5 \\
&1 \times 4 + 1 = 5 \\
&5 - 4 = 1,\ 5 - 1 = 4 \\
&5 \div 4 = 1\ (1)
\end{aligned}
\right.
$$

After the pupils are familiar with all the combinations they may be required to fill out missing numbers ; for example : $3 + \ldots = 5$, $4 \times 1 + \ldots = 5$, $4 \times \ldots + 1 = 5$.

5 is 1 more than 4, 2 more than 3, 3 more than 2, 2 more than 1.

4 is 1 less than 5, 1 more than 3, 2 more than 2, 1 more than 3.

3 is 2 less than 5, 1 more than 2, 2 more than 1.

2 is 3 less than 5, 1 more than 1.

$5 = 5 \times 1$.

$1 = \frac{1}{5} \times 5$ (1 is the fifth part of 5.)

The five consists of unlike numbers, $3 + 2$, and of 2 like numbers and 1 unlike number, $2 + 2 + 1$.

Rapid Work.

$5 - 2 - 2 + 2 - 1 \times 2$, the half, less $1 =$
$2 \times 2 + 1 - 3 \times 1 \times 2 - 3 - 4 = ?$

Combining.

How much must I add to 2 in order to get 5 ?
How much must I take away from 5 in order to get 2 ?
What number is the fifth part of 5 ?
How many times 2 have I added to 1 to get 5 ?

I have taken from a number twice 2 and have 1 left
What is the number?

If to 2 times 2 I add 1, what do I get?

I take 3 times 1 from a number and have 2 left.   What
is the number?

What number shall I add to 2 to get 5?

If I add 1 to a number I get 5.   What is the number?

What must I add to the half of 4 to get 5?

Take 2 times 1, then add it to 2; this lacks how many
of 5?

4 times one third of 3 added to 1 makes what?

Take 3 from 5 and how many will 2 times this lack of 5?

(These combinations must be multiplied to insure readi-
ness and accuracy.   While in the examples above only
those involving 5 are given, review of the numbers already
learned must never be forgotten.)

II. The Applied Number.

How many 3-cent and 2-cent loaves of bread can you
buy for 5 cents?

John received from his father a 3-cent and a 2-cent
piece.   He bought 2 sheets of paper at 2 cents each.   How
much change did he get?

Bertha knit 3 times around, and her sister 2 times
more than she.   How many times around did the sister
knit?

A father divided 5 cherries among his 3 children.   The
youngest got only 1, and the other two each the same
number.   How many did the others get?

Charles gave his 2 sisters each 1 apple, his brother 2
apples, and had 1 for himself.   How many did he have at
first?

The milkman had 5 quarts of milk, and sold 2 quarts to
Mrs. Wilson, 1 quart to Mrs. Rand, and 1 quart to me.
How many quarts did he have left?

John has 2 marbles, David has 3.   How many have both?

John wins 2 from David.   How many has David left?
How many has John now?

How many apples can you buy for 5 cents if 1 apple
costs you 2 cents?   How many cents will you have left?

(These examples must be multiplied, making use of things with which the children are familiar. Continue this practice until they can perform all the operations with absolute accuracy and great rapidity. Whenever a child is in doubt, take him to the blocks and make it clear to him. Or, better, lead him to find out the truth himself by use of the blocks.)

SIXTH STEP.

THE SIX.

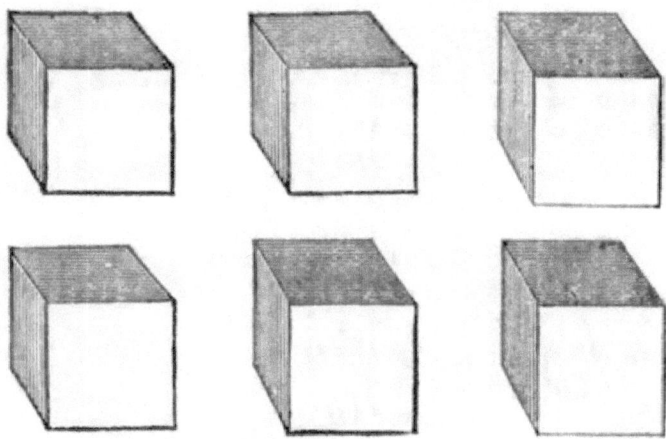

(The pupil is now able to fill out the operations himself according to the method already pursued. If he can do that readily, it may not be necessary to use the objects longer, except when the child is puzzled. Many Germans use no objects in teaching number after the four. Just as soon as the child is familiar with the method, and can grasp the idea of the number without the visible object before him, the objects should be abandoned. But blocks should always be at hand to be used in removing doubt in the child's mind, when a point is not perfectly clear to him.)

I. The Pure Number.—*Measuring.*

o 1
o 1
o 1 $\left\{ \begin{array}{l} 1+1+1+1+1+1=6 \\ 6 \times 1 = 6,\ 1 \times 6 = 6 \end{array} \right.$
o 1
o 1 $6-1-1-1-1-1=1$
o 1 $6+1=6$

(Teach each figure as soon as the child has use for it.)

o o 2 $\left\{ \begin{array}{l} 2+2+2=6.\quad (2+2=4,\ 4+2=6) \\ 3 \times 2 = 6 \end{array} \right.$
o o 2 $6-2-2=2$
o o 2 $6 \div 2 = 3$

o o o 3 $\left\{ \begin{array}{l} 3+3=6 \\ 2 \times 3 = 6 \end{array} \right.$
o o o 3 $6-3=3$
$6 \div 3 = 2$

o o o o 4 $\left\{ \begin{array}{l} 4+2=6,\ 2+4=6 \\ 1 \times 4 + 2 = 6 \end{array} \right.$
o o 2 $6-4=2$
$6 \div 4 = 1\ (2)$

o o o o o 5 $\left\{ \begin{array}{l} 5+1=6,\ 1+5=6 \\ 1 \times 5 + 1 = 6 \end{array} \right.$
o 1 $6-5=1$
$6 \div 5 = 1\ (1)$

$6 = 5+1,\ 4+2,\ 3+3,\ 2+4,\ 1+5$
$5 = 6-1,\ 4+1,\ 3+2,\ 2+3,\ 1+4$
$4 = 6-2,\ 5-1,\ 3+1,\ 2+2,\ 1+3$
$3 = 6-3,\ 5-2,\ 4-1,\ 2+1,\ 1+2$
$2 = 6-4,\ 5-3,\ 4-2,\ 3-1,\ 1+1$
$1 = 6-5,\ 5-4,\ 4-3,\ 3-2,\ 2-1$
$6 = 6 \times 1,\ 3 \times 2,\ 2 \times 3$
$3 = \frac{1}{2} \times 6$ (is half of 6)
$2 = \frac{1}{3} \times 6$
$1 = \frac{1}{6} \times 6.$

Of what 3 like numbers is 6 composed? Of what 3 unlike?

The following tables can be profitably given :

(a) $1 + 5 = 6$
$\quad\; 2 + 4 = 6$
$\quad\; 3 + 3 = 6$
$\quad\; 4 + 2 = 6$
$\quad\; 5 + 1 = 6$

(b) $6 - 1 = 5$
$\quad\; 6 - 2 = 4$
$\quad\; 6 - 3 = 3$
$\quad\; 6 - 4 = 2$
$\quad\; 6 - 5 = 1$
$\quad\; 6 - 6 = 0$

(c) $1 + 2 = 3$
$\quad\; 3 + 2 = 5$
$\quad\; 5 + 1 = 6$

(d) $5 - 2 = 3$
$\quad\; 3 - 2 = 1$

Odd numbers: 1, 3 5;   5, 3, 1

$\quad\; 2 + 2 = 4$
$\quad\; 4 + 2 = 6$

$\quad\quad\quad\quad\quad 6 - 2 = 4$
$\quad\quad\quad\quad\quad 4 - 2 = 2$
$\quad\quad\quad\quad\quad 2 - 2 = 0$

Even numbers: 2, 4, 6;   6, 4, 2.

(e) $1 + 1 = 2$
$\quad\; 1 + 2 = 3$
$\quad\; 1 + 3 = 4$
$\quad\; 1 + 4 = 5$
$\quad\; 1 + 5 = 6$

(f) $6 - 1 = 5$
$\quad\; 5 - 1 = 4$
$\quad\; 4 - 1 = 3$
$\quad\; 3 - 1 = 2$
$\quad\; 2 - 1 = 1$
$\quad\; 1 - 1 = 0.$

(g) $6 = 6$
$\quad\; 6 = 5 + 1$
$\quad\; 6 = 4 + 2$
$\quad\; 6 = 3 + 3$
$\quad\; 6 = 2 + 4$
$\quad\; 6 = 1 + 5$

(h) $6 - 1 = 5$
$\quad\; 6 - 2 = 4$
$\quad\; 6 - 3 = 3$
$\quad\; 6 - 4 = 2$
$\quad\; 6 - 5 = 1$
$\quad\; 6 - 6 = 0.$

(Many other tables can be made embracing multiplication and division as far as the 6. The pupils can easily be led to make these themselves. Dictate numbers, and require the pupils to name or write them promptly, so as to test their knowledge of the order of the numbers, and their ability to make the figures. For example : Write the numbers from 1 to 6. What number comes after 4?

What comes before 4? What comes between 2 and 4?
Express the number that comes after 5. Express the
number between 3 and 5.)

Rapid Work.

$1 \times 2 + 1 \times 2 - 1 \times 1 - 5 + 5 = ?$
$4 + 2 - 3$ is how much less than 6?
$3 - 2 \times 5 + 1 - 4 \times 2 \div 2 + 4 - 5 = ?$
$5 - 4 + 3 \div 2 + 1 \times 2 + 3 = ?$ ·

These should be given orally to the pupils, or written
on the board as rapidly as they are able to work them.
Allow no counting of the fingers or use of objects in this
operation. The pupils must *know* every operation, and
be able to perform rapidly and accurately without any
hesitation. This is a test of the thoroughness of the work.

Combining.

What number can you take 3 times from 6 and twice
from 4?

How many times 1 has half of 6 more than half of 4,
and how much less than 5?

I have taken a number twice away from 6 and have 2
left. What is the number?

How many times is ⅓ of 6 contained in 4? The half of
4 = what part of 6? What number is 3 times 2?

II. The Applied Number.

How many times 1 cent, 2 cents, and 3 cents in 6 cents?
How many quarts in 6 pints?
What will 3 liters of milk cost at 2 cents a liter?
William got 3 tops for 6 cents. What did 1 cost?
I have 6 apples in 3 pockets. How many apples in each
pocket?

How many lead-pencils at 2 cents each can I buy for
6 cents?

I gave each of my 3 sisters 2 oranges. How many
oranges did I give away?

A father divided 6 dollars equally among his 3 children.
How much did each get?

Fanny took 6 cents to the store and bought 2 candies at 2 cents each. How much money did she have left?

Joseph gave Charles 2 marbles, Henry 1, and had 3 left. How many had he at first?

I have 5 dollars and borrow 1 more, and lend 2. How much have I left?

If David earns 2 dimes a day, how much will he earn in 3 days?

Mary gave each of her 5 friends a candy, and had 1 for herself. How much did she have at first?

I have 2 books on the table, 1 on the chair, and 3 in my book-case. How many have I in all?

Jessie buys 3 pints of milk at 2 cents a pint. How much is the cost?

SEVENTH STEP.

THE SEVEN.

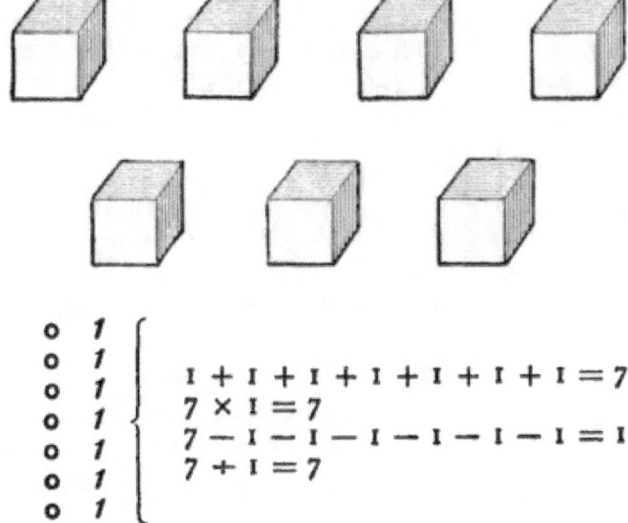

$$1 + 1 + 1 + 1 + 1 + 1 + 1 = 7$$
$$7 \times 1 = 7$$
$$7 - 1 - 1 - 1 - 1 - 1 - 1 = 1$$
$$7 + 1 = 7$$

$$
\begin{array}{ll}
\text{o o} \quad 2 \\
\text{o o} \quad 2 \\
\text{o o} \quad 2 \\
\phantom{\text{o o}} \text{o} \quad 1
\end{array}
\left\{
\begin{array}{l}
2 + 2 + 2 + 1 = 7 \\
3 \times 2 + 1 = 7 \\
7 - 2 - 2 - 2 = 1 \\
7 \div 2 = 3\ (1)
\end{array}
\right.
$$

$$
\begin{array}{ll}
\text{o o o} \quad 3 \\
\text{o o o} \quad 3 \\
\text{o o·o} \quad 1
\end{array}
\left\{
\begin{array}{l}
3 + 3 + 1 = 7 \\
2 \times 3 + 1 = 7 \\
7 - 3 - 3 = 1 \\
7 \div 3 = 2\ (1)
\end{array}
\right.
$$

$$
\begin{array}{ll}
\text{o o o o} \quad 4 \\
\phantom{\text{o}} \text{o o o} \quad 3
\end{array}
\left\{
\begin{array}{l}
4 + 3 = 7;\quad 3 + 4 = 7 \\
1 \times 4 + 3 = 7 \\
7 - 4 = 3 \\
7 \div 4 = 1\ (3)
\end{array}
\right.
$$

$$
\begin{array}{ll}
\text{o o o o o} \quad 5 \\
\phantom{\text{o o o}} \text{o o} \quad 2
\end{array}
\left\{
\begin{array}{l}
5 + 2 = 7;\quad 2 + 5 = 7 \\
1 \times 5 + 2 = 7 \\
7 - 5 = 2 \\
7 \div 5 = 1\ (2)\ *
\end{array}
\right.
$$

$$
\begin{array}{ll}
\text{o o o o o o} \quad 6 \\
\phantom{\text{o o o o o}} \text{o} \quad 1
\end{array}
\left\{
\begin{array}{l}
6 + 1 = 7;\quad 1 + 6 = 7 \\
1 \times 6 + 1 = 7 \\
7 - 6 = 1 \\
7 \div 6 = 1\ (1)
\end{array}
\right.
$$

In what ways can a father divide 7 apples among 2, 3, 4 children?

$$7 = 6 + 1,\ 5 + 2,\ 4 + 3,\ 3 + 4,\ 2 + 5,\ 1 + 6.$$
$$6 = 7 - 1,\ 5 + 1,\ 4 + 2,\ 3 + 3,\ 2 + 4,\ 1 + 5.$$
$$5 = 7 - 2,\ 6 - 1,\ 4 + 1,\ 3 + 2,\ 2 + 3,\ 1 + 4.$$
$$4 = 7 - 3,\ 6 - 2,\ 5 - 1,\ 3 + 1,\ 2 + 2,\ 1 + 3.$$
$$7 = 7 \times 1,\ 1 = \tfrac{1}{7} \text{ of } 7.$$

What like numbers does 7 contain?

(Make tables like those on page 39, and require the pupils to do the same. Follow this course with all succeeding steps.)

---

* I would have the pupils find out how many fives in 7 by use of blocks. Then express $7 \div 5 = 1$ with a remainder of 2. Then write the remainder in parentheses, as: $7 \div 5 = 1\ (2)$. The children will very easily learn that the number in parentheses is the remainder.

Rapid Work.

$3 \times 2 + 1 - 2 \times 1 - 3 \times 3 + 1$?
$2 + 1 + 2 + 1 + 1$? $1 + 2 + 4 - 3 - 2 \times 3$?
$4 + 3 - 1 + 3 + 5 - 1 \div 2 + 4 - 7$?

Combining.

From what number can you take 1 seven times?
What number contains 7 seven times?
To what number must I add 3×2 to get 7?
I take a number 3 times and get 1 less than 7. What is the number?
How many times 1 is 7 greater than the double of 2?

(The double of 2 is 4. 7 is 3 more than 4, and has therefore 3×1 more than 4. Therefore 7 is 3×1 greater than the double of 2.)

II. The Applied Number.

A week has seven days. What is the name of the first, the second, the fifth, the third, the seventh day?
I took a trip lately that lasted just a week; how many days was I on the journey?
How much money did I need for the journey, if I used one dollar a day?
If you put 1 cent in your savings bank each day, how much will that make in a week?
How many threes would that make?
How many quarts in 7 pints?
George was sent by his mother to fetch 2 3-cent loaves of bread. She gave him 7 cents. Was that enough? How much did he have left?
Henry took a 5-cent and a 2-cent piece and bought 3 candles at 2 cents each. How much money should he bring back?

(The teacher must multiply examples of each kind until the pupils have mastered the number. Never leave a number to take up a new one until the former is thoroughly learned.)

EIGHTH STEP.
THE EIGHT.

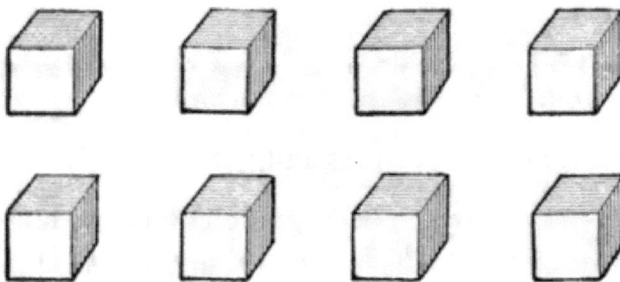

I. The Pure Number.—*Measuring.*

o   *1*
o   *1*
o   *1*
o   *1*
o   *1*
o   *1*
o   *1*
o   *1*

$$1 + 1 + 1 + 1 + 1 + 1 + 1 + 1 = 8$$
$$8 \times 1 = 8$$
$$8 - 1 - 1 - 1 - 1 - 1 - 1 - 1 = 1$$
$$8 \div 1 = 8$$

o o   *2*
o o   *2*
o o   *2*
o o   *2*

$$2 + 2 + 2 + 2 = 8$$
$$4 \times 2 = 8$$
$$8 - 2 - 2 - 2 = 2$$
$$8 \div 2 = 4$$

o o o   *3*
o o o   *3*
o o   *2*

$$3 + 3 + 2 = 8$$
$$2 \times 3 + 2 = 8$$
$$8 - 3 - 3 = 2$$
$$8 \div 3 = 2 \ (2)$$

o o o o   *4*
o o o o   *4*

$$4 + 4 = 8$$
$$2 \times 4 = 8$$
$$8 - 4 = 4$$
$$8 \div 4 = 2$$

o o o o o 5 $\Big\{$ $\begin{aligned} &5 + 3 = 8, \; 3 + 5 = 8 \\ &1 \times 5 + 3 = 8 \\ &8 - 5 = 3 \\ &8 \div 5 = 1 \, (3) \end{aligned}$
   o o o 3

o o o o o o 6 $\Big\{$ $\begin{aligned} &6 + 2 = 8, \; 2 + 6 = 8 \\ &1 \times 6 + 2 = 8 \\ &8 - 6 = 2 \\ &8 \div 6 = 1 \, (2) \end{aligned}$
    o o 2

o o o o o o o 7 $\Big\{$ $\begin{aligned} &7 + 1 = 8, \; 1 + 7 = 8 \\ &1 \times 7 + 1 = 8 \\ &8 - 7 = 1 \\ &8 \div 7 = 1 \, (1) \end{aligned}$
    o 1

$8 = 7 + 1, \, 6 + 2, \, 5 + 3, \, 4 + 4,$ etc.
$7 = 8 - 1, \, 6 + 1, \, 5 + 2, \, 4 + 3,$ etc.
$6 = 8 - 2, \, 5 + 1, \, 4 + 2, \, 3 + 3,$ etc.
$5 = 8 - 3,$ etc., completing the table.
$8 = 2 \times 4, \, 4 \times 2, \, 8 \times 1,$
$1 = \frac{1}{8} \times 8, \, 2 = \frac{1}{4} \times 8, \, 4 = \frac{1}{2} \times 8.$

The 8 consists of 4 equal numbers, for it equals 4×2, and of 2 equal numbers, for it equals 2×4, also of 2 equal and one unequal number, namely, $2 \times 3 + 2$.

Rapid Work.

$8 - 1 - 2 - 1 - 2$?
$1 + 2 + 1 + 2 + 2 - 5$?
$2 \times 2 + 3 + 1 + 4 + 2$?
$4 + 3 - 5 \times 4 \div 2 - 3 \times 7$?

Combining.

What number contains the fourth of 8 three times?

What is the difference between a half of 8 and a half of 6?

What number must I double in order to get 8?

What number must I take 4 times in order to get 8?

What number has 5×1 more than 3?

(The number which has 5×1, or 5, more than 3, is $5 + 3 = 8$.)

Take the third of six 4 times.

II. The Applied Number.

How many twos, threes, and fours are found in 8?
How many gallons in 8 quarts?
How many quarts in 8 pints?
How many weeks in 8 days?

William wanted to buy 4 spools of thread at 2 cents each. How much money must he have? He paid the sum in 2-cent pieces. How many did it take?

If 2 gallons of molasses cost 8 dimes, what will 1 gallon cost?

If 1 bushel of corn costs 8 dimes, what will 1 peck cost?

(1 bushel contains 4 pecks. If 4 pecks cost 8 dimes, 1 peck will cost 2 dimes.)

John has a 5-cent and a 3-cent piece. If he buys 3 tops at 2 cents each, how much money will he have left?

A merchant has a piece of cloth 8 feet long from which he cuts off 2 yards. How much remains?

A yard = 3 feet, 2 yards will = 6 feet. If he cuts off 6 feet there will remain 2 feet.

(In this way, as soon as possible, parts of the tables of compound numbers should be introduced, and the children will thus gradually become familiar with the entire tables. Make examples from every-day life which will be suggested by the errands the children must do or by the employment of their parents. Bring their knowledge of number into immediate, practical use.)

NINTH STEP.

THE NINE.

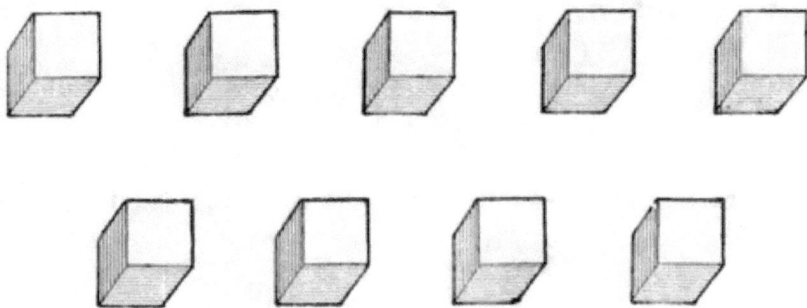

The Pure Number.—*Measuring.*

$$1 + 1 + 1 + 1 + 1 + 1 + 1 + 1 + 1 = 9$$
$$9 \times 1 = 9$$
$$9 - 1 - 1 - 1 - 1 - 1 - 1 - 1 - 1 = 1$$
$$9 \div 1 = 9$$

$$2 + 2 + 2 + 2 + 1 = 9$$
$$4 \times 2 + 1 = 9$$
$$9 - 2 - 2 - 2 - 2 = 1$$
$$9 \div 2 = 4 \ (1)$$

```
o o o  3  ⎧  3 + 3 + 3 = 9
o o o  3  ⎨  3 × 3 = 9
o o o  3  ⎪  9 — 3 — 3 = 3
          ⎩  9 + 3 = 3

o o o o  4  ⎧  4 + 4 + 1 = 9
o o o o  4  ⎨  2 × 4 + 1 = 9
      o  1  ⎪  9 — 4 — 4 = 1
              ⎩  9 ÷ 4 = 2 (1)
```

(Measure 9 with all the other numbers according to the plan followed with the preceding numbers.)

$$9 = 8 + 1, 7 + 2, 6 + 3, \text{etc.}$$
$$8 = 9 - 1, 7 + 1, 6 + 2, \text{etc.}$$
$$7 = 9 - 2, 6 + 1, 5 + 2, \text{etc.}$$
$$6 = 9 - 3, 5 + 1, 4 + 2, \text{etc.}$$

(Continue in the same way; also construct tables as on p. 39.)

$$9 = 9 \times 1, 3 \times 3.$$
$$1 = \tfrac{1}{9} \times 9, 3 = \tfrac{1}{3} \times 9.$$

9 can be separated into—
  3 equal numbers, $3 + 3 + 3$;
  4 equal and 1 unequal numbers, $2 + 2 + 2 + 2 + 1$;
  2 equal and 1 unequal numbers, $4 + 4 + 1$;
  3 unequal numbers, $2 + 3 + 4$;
  2 unequal numbers, $5 + 4$.

Rapid Work.

$$3 \times 3 - 3 - 2 \times 2 - 5 - 1 \times 4?$$
$$1 + 2 + 3 - 3 - 2 + 3 - 4?$$
$$9 ÷ 3 + 4 + 2 - 1 + 4 \times 3?$$

(These should be given very rapidly, and should involve all kinds of operations which the pupils have already had. The pupils should be able to follow as rapidly as the teacher can dictate the combinations, and be ready with the answer as soon as the teacher ceases.)

Combining.

How many times 1 is 4 × 2 less than 3 × 3?

What number can I take four times away from 9 and have 1 left?

What part of the 6 is the third part of 9?

Separate 9 into two unlike numbers, one of which is 1 greater than the other.

II.—The Applied Number.

How many gallons in 9 quarts?

How many weeks in 9 days?

How many 2's, 3's, 4's, and 6's in 9 cents?

Mary had 9 verses to learn. She learned 3 verses each day. How many days did it take her?

Her brother wrote 9 pages in 3 days. How many each day?

What cost 3 sheets of paper if 1 sheet cost 3 cents?

William was to fetch his father 4 sheets of paper, each sheet costing 2 cents. He had 6 cents and 3 cents. How much money must he bring back?

The milkman asks 3 cents a pint for milk. How many pints can I get for 9 cents?

I give Fannie 4 2-cent pieces and a 1-cent piece. She gave her sister 3 cents and her brother 4 cents. How much had she left?

A boy buys 2 lemons at 2 cents each, and 1 orange for 4 cents. He has 1 cent left. How much had he at first?

TENTH STEP.

THE TEN.

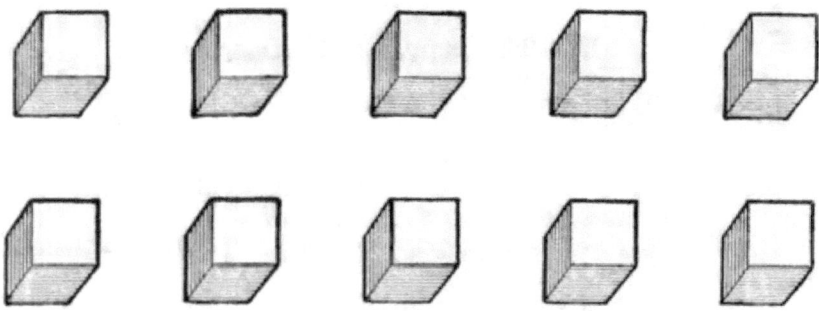

(We have now reached the first number which must be considered as another kind of unity, or another kind of One,—the Ten. So we write again the figure 1, but to show that this 1 contains ten times as much as the first 1, we move it one place to the left, and say, this 1 is a ten. The vacant place of the simple 1 will be indicated with the cipher, so—10. The pupils should be taught as follows :)

Show me 10 fingers. Now 1 finger. Indicate the 1 finger with a figure. Indicate the fingers of both hands with a figure.

(The children are shown how they must write 1 in the ten's place, and the cipher at the right for unit's place. place.)

(Ten splints also may be used, and then bound into a bundle to represent 1 ten. This must be continued until the pupils comprehend the 10 and its relation to the unit.)

Measuring.

(Grube now abandons the writing out of the tables, such as 10 with 1, 10 with 2, 10 with 3, etc., as practised with all preceding numbers. The teacher can require the pupils to do so if he deems it desirable; but it will probably be found unnecessary to go farther in this direction.)

The 10 consists of two equal numbers, 5 + 5; of 5 equal numbers, 2 + 2 + 2 + 2 + 2; of 2 equal and 1 unequal numbers, 3 × 3 + 1; of 4 unequal numbers, 1 + 2 + 3 + 4.

1 is the half of 2	6 is 3 times 2
the third of 3	2 times 3
the fourth of 4, etc.	9 is 9 times 1
2 is the half of 4	3 times 3
the third of 6	8 is 8 times 1
the fourth of 8, etc.	4 times 2
10 is 10 times 1	2 times 4
5 times 2	7 is 7 times 1
2 times 5	5 is 5 times 1
3 is the half of 6	4 is 4 times 1
the third of 9	2 times 2
4 is the half of 8	3 is 3 times 1
5 is the half of 10	2 is 2 times 1
6 is 6 times 1	1 is 1 times 1

What numbers go without remainder into 10, 9, 8, 6, 4?
What are only divided by 1 and themselves? (The prime numbers, 1, 3, 5, 7.)

Rapid Work.

2 × 3 + 2 + 1 − 6 + 5 − 3 × 2 ÷ 5?
10 − 7 × 3 + 1 ÷ 5 × 4 + 1 ÷ 3 + 6?
2 × 2 + 2 + 3 − 7 × 5 ÷ 2 + 4 ÷ 3?
10 − 2 − 1 − 2 − 1 − 2 − 1?
1 + 3 + 3 + 4?

Combining.

What number has 1 more than the double of 3?
How much is 2 × 5 greater than the difference between 3 × 3 and the double of 4?

A father divided 10 apples among his 4 children so that each older received 1 more than the next younger. How many did each receive?

(The 10 consists of the 4 unequal numbers, 1 + 2 + 3 + 4; each is 1 larger than the next below. Therefore the father could give the youngest 1 apple, the next 2, etc.)

N. had learned 4 proverbs. His brother said to him, "I know twice as many again as you and 2 more." How many did he know?

Herman said, "I am 5 times as old as my brother." The brother was 2 years old. How old was Herman?

II.—The Applied Number.

In 10 pints how many quarts?

In 10 days how many weeks and days?

In 10 cents how many 2-cent pieces? 3-cent pieces? 5-cent pieces?

Fred had 6 cents, 3 cents, and 1 cent. He went to a stationer and bought 4 sheets of paper at 2 cents a sheet, and 2 sheets at 1 cent a sheet. Did he have money enough?

Karl had the same amount of money, and bought 3 sheets at 3 cents each. How much did he have left?

How many pints of milk can be bought for 10 cents if 1 pint costs 2 cents? 5 cents?

How many biscuits can I buy for 10 cents at 2 cents each?

A dime has 10 cents. How many 2-cent pieces equal a dime? How many 5-cent pieces?

Ten dimes make a dollar. How many 2-dime pieces in a dollar? 5-dime pieces?

This completes the first school year, and the most important steps in number have been mastered. One year is not too long if the work has been thoroughly done. Of course the child knows only the numbers 1 to 10; but he *knows* them and can use his knowledge; therefore they are of some value to him. Of what use to the child if he count to 100, but could not separate the number 9 into its elements and use them? The process of "measuring" must be thoroughly mastered by the child. He must become so thoroughly acquainted with all of the operations of each step that without hesitation he can perform them. The eye becomes trained by use of the blocks to habits of accuracy, and the child learns to be attentive. By means of the eye and by handling, he gains an idea of the number and its combinations. Thus the objects appeal to his senses, and he is soon able to pass over from the number obtained from concrete things to the abstract. When objects no longer are necessary to give the idea, *the concrete objects must not be named, as that withdraws the attention from the abstract number itself.* Having mastered the abstract number, the child is able to apply it with concrete examples. This will not be difficult, as little examples are made from the every-day relations of life.

At the 10, if not before, the use of objects should be abandoned entirely. The child is now able to gain the abstract idea without the help of objects. Objects become a cumbrance as soon as the child can do without them. Some think they can be abandoned after the 4 or 5. Each teacher must settle the question with the class he may have. When the class are able to get the idea without the objects, then is the time to give them up. Certainly that end will be reached when the 10 is completed.

Reviews must be frequent, and every step must be mastered before proceeding to the next. After knowledge has been obtained by illustration and observation it must be thoroughly memorized.

THE SECOND YEAR: 10–100.

(See Appendix, p. 90.)

OBSERVATIONS.

1. Grube says: " Fingers and lines continue to be used for illustration. One can well say that Nature has given to man the decimal system of number in the hand."*

2. The procedure in the following steps is the same as that given for the smaller numbers. Multiplication and division should be given both as written and oral work, while addition and subtraction need only be oral. The pupils must continue the " measuring" of each new number by the numbers from 1 to 10 until the greatest mechanical skill is reached. This mechanical skill is connected with the greatest self-activity on the part of the pupil.

3. For the operations with the pure as well as the applied numbers, a greater diversity in the manner of expression in the examples can be employed, in order that the pupil may become more and more free from the formulas of the earlier work. Applied examples should be gathered from the pupil's surroundings, from material with which he is familiar. Here is an excellent opportunity to lead the pupil to invent examples, and the privilege of giving an example to the class may be accorded to the pupil first solving a given example. This originating of examples will not be difficult, because the pupil always proceeds from the preceding step, and only adds to the already known.

---

* While Grube continued to use objects to illustrate the number, his modern followers abandon them, as we have already shown. Simple lines may be used profitably, as the following pages illustrate, to show the relations of units to tens, etc. But the numbers do not need to be longer taught by the use of objects, as heretofore.

ELEVENTH STEP.

THE ELEVEN.

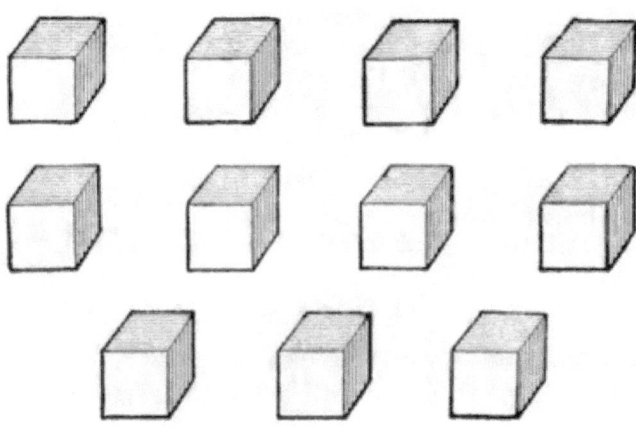

I.—The Pure Number.

10 times one or 10 ones make 1 ten.

If I have 10 ones taken together, I have 1 ten and no (o) ones or units besides.

| | | | | | | | | | | = 1 ten and o ones = 10.

If another one is added, it belongs to the second ten.

| | | | | | | | | | | 10 + 1 = 11.
|

What is the 1 at the right? What the 1 at the left? Where does the one (unit) belong? How many ones must be added in order to make the second ten full? What do we call 1 ten and 1 one in one word? What is the 11?

Oral.

Measure with 1.

1 + 1 + 1 + etc. = 11. (1 + 1 = 2, 2 + 1 = 3, 3 + 1 = 4, etc.)

11 × 1 = 11.

11 − 1 − 1 − 1, etc. = 1. (11 − 1 = 10, 10 − 1 = 9, 9 − 1 = 8, etc.)

11 ÷ 1 = 11.

Measure with 2.

2 + 2 + 2 + 2 + 2 + 1 = 11.

5 × 2 + 1 = 11.

11 − 2 − 2 − 2 − 2 − 2 = 1.

11 ÷ 2 = 5 (1).

Measure with 10.

10 + 1 = 11.

1 × 10 + 1 = 11 (1 ten + 1 one = 11).

11 − 10 = 1.

11 ÷ 10 = 1 (1) (In 11 is 1 ten + 1 one).

(Each pupil gets by this means a principle, and as he knows the course to follow, all assistance from the teacher must cease.)

All numbers hereafter are measured only by the numbers from 1 to 10.

Written.

| | | | | | | | | | = 10 + 1 = 11
|

11 = 11 × 1	11 ÷ 1 = 11
5 × 2 + 1	2 = 5 (1)
3 × 3 + 2	3 = 3 (2)
2 × 4 + 3	4 = 2 (3)
2 × 5 + 1	5 = 2 (1)
1 × 6 + 5	6 = 1 (5)
1 × 7 + 4	7 = 1 (4)
1 × 8 + 3	8 = 1 (3)
1 × 9 + 2	9 = 1 (2)
1 × 10 + 1	10 = 1 (1)

Comparison (oral).

$11 = 10 + 1, 9 + 2, 8 + 3$, etc.

$11 = 11 \times 1, 1 = \frac{1}{11} \times 11$ (1 is $\frac{1}{11}$ of 11).

Form 11 from 3 equal and 1 unequal number.

    4 equal and 2 unequal numbers.

    5 equal and 1 unequal number.

    4 unequal numbers.

Rapid Work.

I have 6 cents, 3 cents, 1 cent, and 1 cent, and give away 4 cents, 2 cents, and 3 cents.   How much have I left ?

$$11 - 2 - 3 - 4 + 3 - 1 \div 2 \times 5?$$
$$11 - 2 - 1 - 2 - 1 - 2 - 1?$$
$$2 \times 5 + 1 - 9 \times 4 + 3 - 7 + 4?$$
$$11 - 5 \div 3 + 8 \div 5 \times 4 - 3 \times 2 + 1?$$

(Let all the possible combinations within the 11 be given orally until the pupil can reckon as rapidly as the teacher can give them.)

Combining.

How many 1's must I add to 5×2 to get 11 ?

From what number must I take 3×3 to get 2 ?

How often can I take the fourth part of 8 away from 11?

What number is 1 ten greater than 1 ?

What is the difference between 4×2 and 11 ?

II. The Applied Number.

11 cents = 3 three-cent pieces and 1 two-cent piece.

11 pints contain 5 quarts and 1 pint.

11 days = 1 week and 4 days.

N. made a journey of 11 days and used just 11 dollars. How much was that per day ?

B. used on a journey 11 dollars.   If he used 1 dollar a day, how many days was he on the way?

Fanny had 2 five-cent pieces and 1 cent.   She bought 2 lead pencils at 3 cents each and 2 at 2 cents each.   How much money had she left?

A boy was given $2 \times 4 + 3$ cents for doing errands.   He put 5 cents + 3 cents in his bank, spent 2 cents for candy and gave the rest to his sister. How much did he give her?

If milk costs 4 cents a quart, how many quarts can I buy for 11 cents and how many cents would I have left?

A mother gave one son 3 × 2 cents. and another 2 × 2 + 1 cent. How much did she give both?

Henry had 5 apples, John gave him 2 and William gave him 2 × 2. How many had he then?

Mr A. had 11 nuts which he divided among four boys. To the first he gave two and to the others each an equal number. How many did each of the others receive?

TWELFTH STEP.

THE TWELVE.

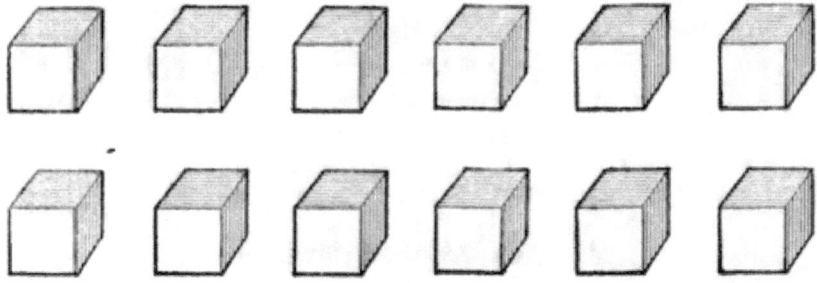

I. The Pure Number.

| | | | | | | | | | | | = 10 + 2 = 12
| |

Oral.

1 + 1 + 1 + 1, etc., = 12
12 × 1 = 12
12 − 1 − 1 − 1, etc., = 1
12 ÷ 1 = 12

$$2 + 2 + 2 + 2 + 2 + 2 = 12$$
$$6 \times 2 = 12$$
$$12 - 2 - 2 - 2 - 2 - 2 = 2$$
$$12 \div 2 = 6$$

$$3 + 3 + 3 + 3 = 12$$
$$4 \times 3 = 12$$
$$12 - 3 - 3 - 3 = 3$$
$$12 \div 3 = 4$$

(Measure in the same manner by all the numbers as far as 10.)

Written.

$12 = 12 \times 1$	$12 \div 1 = 12$
6×2	$2 = 6$
4×3	$3 = 4$
3×4	$4 = 3$
$2 \times 5 + 2$	$5 = 2 (2)$
2×6	$6 = 2$
$1 \times 7 + 5$	$7 = 1 (5)$
$1 \times 8 + 4$	$8 = 1 (4)$
$1 \times 9 + 3$	$9 = 1 (3)$
$1 \times 10 + 2$	$10 = 1 (2)$
(1 ten + 2 units.)	(In 12 are 1 ten and 2 units.)

$12 = 11 + 1,\ 10 + 2,\ 9 + 3$, etc.
12 is 1 more than 11, 2 more than 10, etc.
1 is the twelfth part of 12.
2 is the sixth part of 12.
3 is the fourth part of 12.
4 is the third part of 12.
6 is half of 12.

From what equal numbers can 12 be formed? From what unequal numbers?

Form 12 from 3 numbers, the first of which is 2 and the following always increasing by 2.

Rapid Work.*

$$2 \times 2 + 2 \times 2 \div 4 - 1?$$
$$2 + 3 + 3 + 2 + 2 - 4 + 4 + 4 \times 2?$$

From 12 apples, one half are eaten, then half the remainder, then 1. How many remained?

From 12 cents take away 1 three-cent and 1 two-cent piece, then again 1 three-cent and 1 two-cent piece. How much remains.

$$12 - 6 + 3 - 5 + 7 - 1 \div 2 - 3?$$
$$10 + 2 \div 4 \times 2 + 3 \div 3 + 9?$$
$$8 + 2 + 2 + 3 \div 2 \times 6 - 11 + 7?$$
$$5 \times 2 + 2 + 6 + 7 \div 3 \times 4 - 7?$$
$$6 - 5 \times 12 - 9 \times 3 - 1 + 4?$$

Combining.

The third part of 12 is what part of 8? The half of 12 is how many times 3?

What is the difference between $\frac{1}{3}$ of 12 and $\frac{1}{2}$ of 10?

12 is 3 times what number?

What number must I subtract from 12 to get 9?

(As $9 + 3 = 12$, 3 must be taken from 12 to get 9.)

What number subtracted from 12 leaves 4?

II. The Applied Number.

12 things make a dozen.

12 months make a year.

What part of a dozen are 6 things?

What part of a year are 6 months?

3 months = a quarter of a year.

4 months = a third of a year,

How many gallons in 12 quarts?

How many quarts in 12 pints?

How many sixes, fours, threes, twos in 12?

---

* It must not be forgotten that the exercises of "Rapid Work" are to be worked as fast as the teacher dictates, and that it is oral work only. The object is to gain facility in head-work. All idea of parenthetical expressions is excluded here.

In a month there are four weeks. If a boy earns 12 dollars a month, how much does he earn per week?

A father pays 2 dollars a month for his son's lessons. How much is that for 3 months? How much for 6 months?

Charles divided 12 cents equally among 4 poor boys. How much did each receive?

How many sheets of paper at 3 cents each can you buy for 12 cents?

(As many times as I have 3 cents I get a sheet of paper. 12 cents = 4 × 3 cents, so I get 4 × 1 sheet, or 4 sheets.)

Illustrated.

```
| | |   .  .   .  .   .  o
| | |   .  .   .  .   .  o
| | |   .  .   .  .   .  o
| | |   .  .   .  .   .  o
```

A foot contains 12 inches. How many inches in ⅓ of a foot? ⅙? ¼?

What part of a foot is 4 inches? 6 inches?

A troy pound contains 12 ounces. What part of a pound is 3 ounces? 4 ounces?

If a top costs 3 cents, a whistle 2 cents, and a ball 7 cents, how much do all cost?

John takes a dime and a 2-cent piece to the store and buys 4 lead pencils at 2 cents each, and a sponge for 3 cents. How much money had he left?

John has 8 cents; how much more must he earn to have a dozen cents?

THIRTEENTH STEP.

THE THIRTEEN.

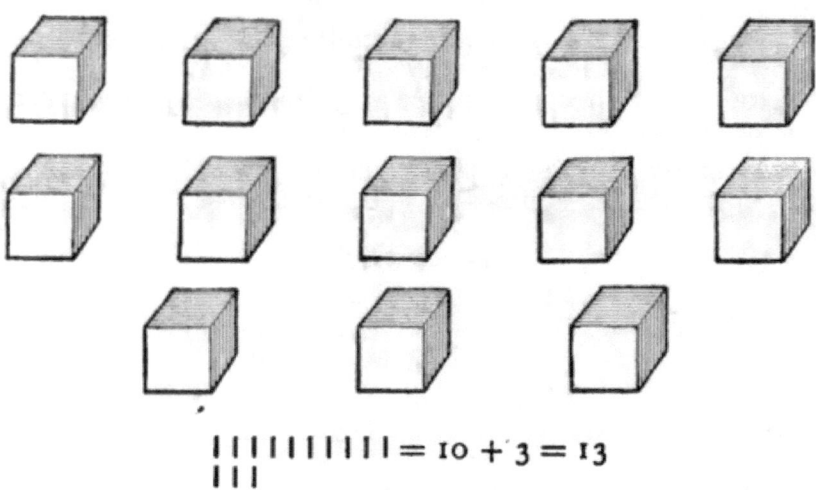

$$\mid\mid\mid\mid\mid\mid\mid\mid\mid\mid = 10 + 3 = 13$$
$$\mid\mid\mid$$

(Measuring and rapid work the same as before.)

Combining.

Make 13 by multiplying 3's and 2's.

$$(3 \times 3 + 2 \times 2 = 9 + 4 = 13.)$$

How does the difference between 13 and 9 compare with the difference between 12 and 8?

Subtract 6 from 13.

$$(13 - 6 = 7, \text{ for } 13 - 3 = 10 \text{ and } 10 - 3 = 7.)$$

What number $= 7 + 6$?
What number $= 8 + 5$?
What number must I add to 4×3 to get 13?

II. The Applied Number.

Mary has a 10-cent and a 3-cent piece, with which she buys 4 oranges at 3 cents each.   How much has she left?

A gentleman divides 13 apples among some children, giving the first child 3 apples, and the others 2 apples each.   How many children were there?

FOURTEENTH STEP.
THE FOURTEEN.

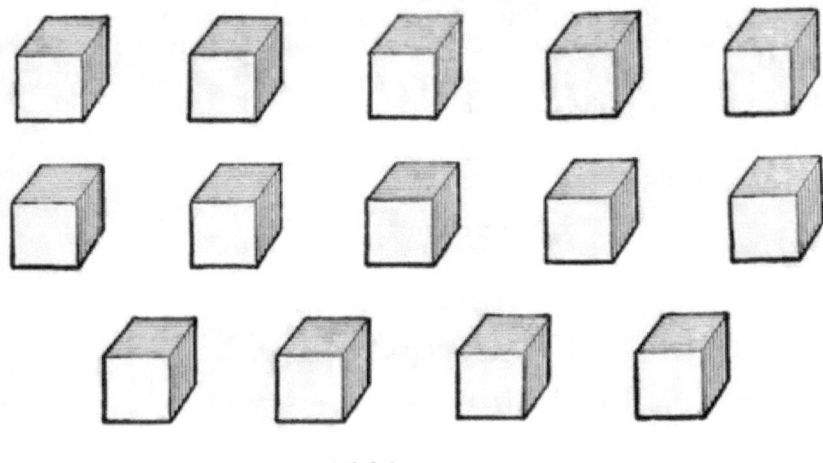

$$| | | | | | | | | | = 10 + 4 = 14.$$
$$| | | |$$

What number must I double to get 7 × 2?

2 sparrows lit upon a tree, and then 2 more, and 3, and 3 and 2 × 2; 3 + 4 + 5 soon flew away. How many remained?

I have taken a certain number 3 times away from 14, and have 2 left. What is the number?

(If I have 2 left, I must have taken 12 away; 12 is 3 × 4, so I have taken 4 three times away from 14 if I have 2 remainder.)

II.—The Applied Number.

14 days = 2 weeks.

14 cents = 7 two-cent pieces, 4 three-cent and 1 two-cent piece, etc.

14 things = 1 dozen and 2 things.

14 months = 1 year and 2 months.

If I travel for 2 weeks, and spend 1 dollar each day, how much will my journey cost?

What will 1 dozen and 2 pencils cost at 1 cent each?

How many sheets of paper can I buy for 1 dime and 4 cents, if a sheet costs 2 cents?

Marie knit in 1 year 7 pair of stockings. How many dozen did she knit, and how many stockings over?

If I sell 7 pigs at 2 dollars each, how much do I receive?

A man buys 14 pounds of sugar for 1 dollar and 4 dimes. What does 1 pound cost?

FIFTEENTH STEP.

THE FIFTEEN.

I.—The Pure Number.

| | | | | | | | | | | 10 + 5 = 15.
| | | | |

How many units belong to the second 10? How many are still lacking to make the second 10 full? Write 15 in dots so that 5 always stand together.

$$\begin{matrix} \cdot & \cdot & \cdot & \cdot & \cdot \\ \cdot & \cdot & \cdot & \cdot & \cdot \end{matrix} \Big| \begin{matrix} \cdot & \cdot & \cdot & \cdot & \cdot \end{matrix}$$

Write these fives under each other.

$$\left.\begin{matrix} \cdot & \cdot & \cdot & \cdot & \cdot \\ \cdot & \cdot & \cdot & \cdot & \cdot \\ \cdot & \cdot & \cdot & \cdot & \cdot \end{matrix}\right\} 3 \times 5$$

Write them so that 3 stand in a row.

$$\left.\begin{matrix} \cdot & \cdot & \cdot \\ \cdot & \cdot & \cdot \\ \cdot & \cdot & \cdot \\ \cdot & \cdot & \cdot \\ \cdot & \cdot & \cdot \end{matrix}\right\} 5 \times 3$$

Of what unequal numbers does 15 consist? Of what 3 unequal numbers?

What is the difference between 15 and 8?

(*a.* I observe how much I must add to 8 to get 15. 8 + 2 = 10, 10 + 5 = 15, 8 + 7 = 15. The difference between 8 and 15 is 7.

b. I take 8 from 15; 15 − 5 = 10, 10 − 3 = 7, 15 − 8 = 7.) *

In what number is found an entire and a half ten ?

What 5 numbers give the sum of 15 ?

Each following of these 5 numbers is to be 1 larger than the preceding.   1 + 2 + 3 + 4 + 5.

At Easter a mother divided among her 5 children boiled eggs according to age, so that each older got 1 egg more than the next younger.   The middle child in age got 3 eggs.   How many did each of the others get? How many eggs were distributed ?

II.—The Applied Number.

Compare 1 doz. with 15.

    1 doz. = 4 × 3 things.

      15 = 5 × 3 things = 1 doz. + 3 things.

        15 cents = 1 dime + 5 cents.

        15 days = 2 weeks + 1 day.

Mary buys 15 pints of milk ; how many quarts does she buy ?

I sent a friend 3 five-cent postage stamps.   How much are they worth ?   I bought 4 two-cent, 2 one-cent, and 1 five-cent stamp.   How much did all cost ?

---

* A strong point practised by the Germans in their arithmetical calculations is here illustrated.   They make the 10 an important factor in all operations.   This will be more fully discussed later.

SIXTEENTH STEP.

THE SIXTEEN.

I.—The Pure Number.

❘ ❘ ❘ ❘ ❘ ❘ ❘ ❘ ❘ ❘　10 + 6 = 16.
❘ ❘ ❘ ❘ ❘ ❘

How many ones, twos, threes in the second 10?
Divide the 16 lines into twos, fours, eights.

❘ ❘ ❘ ❘ ❘ ❘ ❘ ❘ ❘ ❘ ❘ ❘
❘ ❘ ❘ ❘ ❘ ❘

. . . .
. . . . . .

Write 16 in twos perpendicularly.

	In fours.	In eights.

8 × 2

4 × 4　　　2 × 8

Where do we find equal numbers of points horizontally and perpendicularly?

(Many pupils will now be able to construct a square and divide it into equal parts.)

Rapid Work.

How many are 2 + 2 + 2 + 2 + 2 + 2 + 2 + 2?
How many are 1 + 2 + 3 + 1 + 2 + 3 + 1 + 2 less than 16?
How many are 16 − 3 − 3 + 2 − 3?
16 + 4 + 3 + 2 ÷ 3 × 5 − 9 + 10?

Combining.

How do you find the half of 16?
(16 = 1 ten + 6 units.　½ of 1 ten is 5 units, ½ of 6 units

is 3 units. 5 units + 3 units = 8 units. Therefore $\frac{1}{2}$ of 16 = 8.)

A had 6 dimes. B said, " If you take $\frac{1}{3}$ of your money 8 times, you will have as much as I." How much had B?

(B's amount was $8 \times \frac{1}{3}$ of A's; $\frac{1}{3} \times 6$ dimes [the third part] = 2 dimes. Therefore B had 8×2 dimes = 16 dimes.)

A.   B.

I I | I I | I I

What number = $2 \times \frac{1}{4}$ of 16?
What part of 16 is that?

($\frac{1}{4}$ of 16 = 4, $2 \times 4 = 8$. Therefore 8 is $2 \times \frac{1}{4}$ of 16. $16 = 2 \times 8$. Therefore $8 = \frac{1}{2}$ of 16.)

$8 \{ \cdots \\ \cdots \}$ $8 \{ \cdots \\ \cdots \}$ $\} 16$

II.—The Applied Number.

(Applications of the denominations of compound numbers should be made as soon as a number embraced in any table is reached. If possible, place the various measures in the hands of the pupils and let them measure out the various denominations. Dots may be used to give a picture of the relations of the various denominations to each other. In this way all the tables of compound numbers will be gradually and intelligently learned.)

In 1 bushel there are 4 pecks. How many bushels in 16 pecks?

A pound avoirdupois contains 16 ounces. How many ounces in half a pound? What part of a pound is 4 ounces?

If a pail holds 2 gallons, how many pailfuls will 16 gallons make?

A farmer sold 16 bushels of potatoes at half a dollar a bushel. How much does he get for all?

SEVENTEENTH STEP.

THE SEVENTEEN.

I.—The Pure Number.

| | | | | | | | | | 10 + 7 = 17.
| | | | | | |

How many ones have we now? How many are lacking of 2 full tens? How many more has the first row than the second?

With what numbers can we measure the 17? Begin with 16.

$$17 = 16 + 1$$
$$15 + 2$$
$$14 + 3, \text{ etc.}$$

Of how many ones, twos, etc., does 17 consist?

$$17 = 17 \times 1$$
$$8 \times 2 + 1$$
$$5 \times 3 + 2$$
$$4 \times 4 + 1, \text{ etc.}$$

Make 17 from 3 equal and 1 unequal number.

$$17 = 3 \times 5 + 2$$
$$3 \times 4 + 5$$
$$3 \times 3 + 8, \text{ etc.}$$

Make 17 from 4 equal and unequal numbers, also from 5 equal and 1 unequal number.

Rapid Work.

$$17 - 2 - 2 - 2 - 2 - 2 - 2 - 2?$$
$$17 - 3 - 3 - 3, \text{ etc.}$$
$$17 - 4 - 4 - 4, \text{ etc.}$$
$$17 - 5 - 5, \text{ etc.}$$

$1 + 2 + 3 + 4 + 5$ lacks how many of 17?
2 threes, 1 five, and 1 three lacks how many of 17?
$17 - 7 \div 5 \times 8 \div 4 - 1 \times 5$?
$3 \times 5 + 2 - 1 \div 4 + 8 + 5 - 1$?

Combining.

How many ones must I add to 3×5 to get 17?
How many ones must I add to 5×3 to get 17? (Answer: The same.)
What relation has 4×4 and 3×5 to 17?
I have taken 4×4 from 17 and obtained just the same as if I had taken double another number from 17. Of what number must I have taken the double?

II.—The Applied Number.

How many pounds in 17 ounces?
Four brothers divided 17 cents so that the oldest had 1 one more than the others. How many cents did he get?
In 17 quarts how many gallons?
Charles had a dime, a five-cent piece, and a cent. How much did he lack of 17 cents?
A milkman had 2 cans of milk, each holding 10 gallons. One was full, and the other had 7 gallons in it. How many gallons had he in both? How many gallons did the second can lack of being full?
Henry divided 17 cents equally among 5 poor children. How many cents did each get, and how many had he left?
If Charles can walk 3 miles in an hour, how long will it take him to walk 17 less 2 miles?

EIGHTEENTH STEP.

THE EIGHTEEN.

I.—The Pure Number.

❘ ❘ ❘ ❘ ❘ ❘ ❘ ❘ ❘ ❘   10 + 8 = 18.
❘ ❘ ❘ ❘ ❘ ❘ ❘ ❘

Write the number 18 in dots so that 2 always come to·gether.

. .   . .

How many pairs has the first ten?   How many pairs are lacking in the second ten?

Write the number 18 so that 3 lines come together.

❘ ❘ ❘   ❘ ❘ ❘   ❘ ❘ ❘
❘ ❘ ❘   ❘ ❘ ❘   ❘ ❘ ❘

How many threes and how many sixes has the 18?
Write the sixes in horizontal lines.

❘ ❘ ❘ ❘ ❘ ❘
❘ ❘ ❘ ❘ ❘ ❘
❘ ❘ ❘ ❘ ❘ ❘

Write the 18 in fives.

. . . .
. . . .
. . . .
. .

Of what 2 equal numbers does 18 consist?   Of what 3 6, 9?
Of what 3 equal together with 1 unequal number?
Of what 4 equal together with 1 unequal number?

Rapid Work.

Add rapidly 2 twos, 1 three, 2 twos, 1 five and 1 two.

$$2 + 2 + 2 + 3 + 3 + 3 + 3?$$

Count upwards by twos, commencing with 2 (2, 4, 6, etc.) to 18.
The same backwards.
The same commencing with 3.   Also backwards.

Combining.

Of what number is 18 sixfold?

What is the number of which 12 is twofold and 18 threefold?

What part of 12 is this number? Of 18?

What part of 12 is 18 greater than 12?

What number must I multiply by 3 to get 18?

How much greater is the double of 9 than the double of 8, 7, 6?

II.—The Applied Number.

If a pound of meat costs 9 cents, how many pounds can be had for 18 cents?

How many weeks are there in 18 days?

If Mr. A works 3 weeks at 1 dollar a day, how much does he earn?

Fred was sent to market with 18 dimes. He bought 4 pounds of veal at 1 dime a pound; 6 pounds of beefsteak at 2 dimes a pound; cabbage for 1 dime. How much money had he left?

If a child is 18 months old, how many years old is it?

A farmer had 18 pecks of clover seed. How many bushels had he?

NINETEENTH STEP.

THE NINETEEN.

I.—The Pure Number.

1.

| | | | | | | | | | $10 + 9 = 19.$
| | | | | | | | |

What have we now?

We have 1 ten and 9.

How many does this lack of 2 full tens?

It lacks but 1 and then the second ten is complete.

Write 19 in lines of 2 each.

```
| |   | |   | |   | |   | |
| |   | |   | |   | |   |
```

Write the ten in twos and the nine in threes.

```
 .  .    .  .    .  .    .  .    .  .
   .  .    .  .    .    .  .  .
```

Write in lines of 5 each.

```
| | | | |     | | | | |
| | | | |     | | | |
```

How many fives in 19? sixes? sevens? eights? Illustrate these by lines.

```
| | | | | |
| | | | | |
| | | | | |
|
```

```
| | | | | | |
| | | | | | |
| | | | |
        etc.
```

Rapid Work.

$$1 + 2 + 2 + 2 + 2 + 2 + 2 + 2 + 2 + 2?$$
$$19 - 1 - 2 - 2, \text{ etc.}$$

(An excellent practice is found in starting from a given number and counting upward as far as 19 and backward by twos, threes, fours, etc. For example: by twos from 3; as, 3, 5, 7, 9, 11, 13, 15, 17, 19; 19, 17, 15, etc.: or by threes from 4; as, 4, 7, 10, 13, 16, 19; 19, 16, 13, etc. This must be done with greatest rapidity and without hesitation.)

Combining.

5 times what number + 4 times what number make together 19?

3 times a number + 1 = 19. What is the number?
6 times a number + 1 = 19. What is the number?
How can I divide 19 apples among 6 children so that at least 5 get the same number? How many would the sixth get?

II.—The Applied Number.

Gussie had 2 dollars, or 20 dimes. George had 1 dollar and 9 dimes, or 19 dimes. How much does George lack of having as much as Gussie?

"My little brother," said Anna, "is 1½ years old;" "And mine," said Bertha, "is just 1 month older." How many months old was the latter? How much over 1 year?

A cloak requires 3 yards of cloth, each yard costing 6 dollars. Reckon also 1 dollar for the velvet collar. What will the cloak cost?

TWENTIETH STEP.

THE TWENTY.

I.

| | | | | | | | | | $10 + 10 = 20.$
| | | | | | | | | |

Now how many tens have we?

Show me 20 fingers. (Let two children hold up both hands.)

Here are twenty sticks. How many bundles of tens can we make from them? We bind them together and have what number?

Write 20 so that the lines fall in twos.

|| || || || ||
|| || || || ||

How many fours are there?

The 10 can be separated in two equal parts; how many the 20?

$$\left.\begin{matrix} \cdot\ \cdot\ \cdot\ \cdot\ \cdot \\ \cdot\ \cdot\ \cdot\ \cdot\ \cdot \\ \cdot\ \cdot\ \cdot\ \cdot\ \cdot \\ \cdot\ \cdot\ \cdot\ \cdot\ \cdot \end{matrix}\right\} 4 \times 5 = 20$$

How many points in one of these horizontal lines ? In one of the perpendicular lines ?

Now write 4 dots in a horizontal line; how many rows are there ?

$$5 \times 4 = 20$$

Of what equal numbers does 20 consist ?

$$20 \times 1, \ 10 \times 2, \ 5 \times 4, \ 4 \times 5, \ 2 \times 10.$$

Of what number is 20 the double ? The fourfold ? The fivefold ? The tenfold ?

What part of 20 is 2, 4, 5, 10?

Measure with 1.

1, 2, 3, 4, 5, 6, (In which ten are we? How many does it lack of being full?), 7, 8, 9, 10, 11, 12, 13, 14, 15.

(How many have we in the second ten? How many in all? How many ones must we take to fill the second ten?)

$$20 \times 1 = 20.$$

20, 19, 18, 17, (Stop! how many ones must we still take away before we get to the first ten?) etc.

$$20 \div 1 = 20.$$

I can take 1 away from 20 twenty times, or 1 is contained in 20 twenty times.

Measure with 2.

2, 4, 6, 8, 10, 12, (How many times 2 have we now?) 14, 16, (How many now?) 18, 20.

$$10 \times 2 = 20.$$

20, 18, 16, 14, etc.

$$20 \div 2 = 10.$$

Measure with 3.

3, 6, 9, 12, 15, 18, (How many must we still add to get 20?) 20.

$$6 \times 3 + 2 = 20.$$

How many times can I take 3 from 20?
(As often as I take 3 away, we will count a finger.)
20, 17, 14, 11, 8, 5, 2.

$$20 \div 3 = 6 \ (2), \text{ etc.}$$

$20 = 20 \times 1$	$20 \div 1 = 20$
10×2	$2 = 10$
$6 \times 3 \ (2)$	$3 = 6 \ (2)$
5×4	$4 = 5$
4×5	$5 = 4$
$3 \times 6 \ (2)$	$6 = 3 \ (2)$
$2 \times 7 \ (6)$	$7 = 2 \ (6)$
$2 \times 8 \ (4)$	$8 = 2 \ (4)$
$2 \times 9 \ (2)$	$9 = 2 \ (2)$
2×10	$10 = 2$

Rapid Work.

How much is $(2 \times 2) + (2 \times 2) + (2 \times 2) + (2 \times 2) + (2 \times 2)$?

How much is $(3 \times 2) + (3 \times 2) + (3 \times 2)$ less than 20?

Subtract 4, 3, 2, 1 from 20 and again 4, 3, 2, 1, and how many remain?

$20 - 13 - 6$?

$20 - 11$? 9? 8? 6? 4?

How many dozen and how many units in 20?

$$20 \div 2 + 5 + 5 \times 3 + 1 \times 2 =$$
$$20 - 4 \div 4 + 6 \times 2 - 12 \div 8 ?$$

Combining.

4 times $5 = 2$ times what number?

5 times $4 = 4$ times what number?

What is the difference between 4×5 and 5×4? Between 4×5 and 4×4?

A gardener divided 20 apples among children so that he gave each child the same number and still had 2 to save for Fred. How many did each child get?

(If Fred received 2, there remained 18 to divide. 18 can be divided into 3 equal parts, etc.)

II.—The Applied Number.

20 things = a score.
20 cents = 2 dimes.
How many weeks in 20 days?
How many pounds in 20 ounces?
Charles had 20 cents to spend. He bought 3 apples at 2 cents each, a ball at 10 cents, gave his sister 2 cents, and kept the balance. How much did he keep?
James is 20 years old and his brother Chester is 3 years younger than he, while his cousin John is 6 years younger than Chester. How old is John?
2 dimes is how many times 5 cents?
20 cents equal how many 2-cent pieces?
A farmer had 20 pecks of corn. How many bushels had he?
A board is 20 inches long. How much of it must I saw off in order to leave just a foot?
A merchant found just 20 feet in a piece of cloth. How many yards did the piece contain?
A milkman had 2 ten-gallon cans full of milk. He sold 11 gallons in the morning, and the rest in the evening. How much did he sell in the evening?
If I can walk 4 miles in an hour, how long will it take me to walk 20 miles?
How long if I walk 5 miles an hour?
In the morning there were 9 boys and 11 girls at school. In the afternoon 3 pupils stayed out. How many were there in the afternoon?
If I pay 1 dollar for 2 bushels of potatoes, how much must I pay for 20 bushels?
In a score of years how many birthdays will you have?

(In this manner all the following numbers are treated, and the teacher will now be prepared to continue the

course himself. A written preparation should be made
in order that nothing be omitted, and that the pupil be
induced in the best manner to prepare the exercises himself. Especial attention should be given to such numbers
as 24, 30, 50, 60, etc., which are more often applied.
Such numbers as 23, 29, etc., need but little attention.
Two or three steps more will suffice.)

THIRTIETH STEP.

THE THIRTY.

I.—The Pure Number.

$$| | | | | | | | | | \quad 10 + 10 + 10 = 30.$$
$$| | | | | | | | | |$$
$$| | | | | | | | | |$$

(3 times the fingers of 2 hands.)
If I add 1 to the 29 the third ten will be full.
3 tens taken together is called 30.

Measure with 1.

Count by ones upwards: 1, 2, 3, 4, 5, 6, 7, (Stop! a
pupil says: "We are in the first ten; it lacks 3 of being
full, and 20 more of 30.") 8, 9, 10, 11, 12, 13, (We are in
the second ten, etc.) 14, 15, etc.

$$30 \times 1 = 30.$$

Count downwards : 30, 29, 28, (We are in the third ten ;
from the third ten 2 have been taken away.) 27, 26, etc.

$$30 \div 1 = 30.$$

Measure with 2.

2, 4, 6, 8, 10, 12, 14, (We are in the second ten ; it lacks

3 twos of being full, and 5 twos more of completing the 3 tens or thirty.) etc.

$$15 \times 2 = 30.$$

Count downwards with 2: 30, 28, 26, 24, (We are in the third ten, have taken 3 twos from the third ten and there remain 2 twos in the third ten.)

$$30 \div 2 = 15.$$

Continue with the other numbers.

Measure with 10.

$$10 + 10 = 20, \ 20 + 10 = 30.$$
$$3 \times 10 = 30.$$
$$30 - 10 = 20, \ 20 - 10 = 10.$$
$$30 \div 10 = 3.$$

$$\left.\begin{array}{l} \bullet \ \bullet \ \bullet \ \bullet \ \bullet \ \bullet \ \bullet \ \bullet \ \bullet \ \bullet \\ \bullet \ \bullet \ \bullet \ \bullet \ \bullet \ \bullet \ \bullet \ \bullet \ \bullet \ \bullet \\ \bullet \ \bullet \ \bullet \ \bullet \ \bullet \ \bullet \ \bullet \ \bullet \ \bullet \ \bullet \end{array}\right\} \ 3 \times 10 = 30.$$

$30 = 30 \times 1$	$30 \div 1 = 30$
15×2	$2 = 15$
10×3	$3 = 10$
$7 \times 4 \ (2)$	$4 = 7 \ (2)$
6×5	$5 = 6$
5×6	$6 = 5$
$4 \times 7 \ (2)$	$7 = 4 \ (2)$
$3 \times 8 \ (6)$	$8 = 3 \ (6)$
$3 \times 9 \ (3)$	$9 = 3 \ (3)$
3×10	$10 = 3$

Divide the dots into twos:

$$\left.\begin{array}{l} \bullet \ \bullet \mid \bullet \ \bullet \mid \bullet \ \bullet \mid \bullet \ \bullet \mid \bullet \ \bullet \\ \bullet \ \bullet \mid \bullet \ \bullet \mid \bullet \ \bullet \mid \bullet \ \bullet \mid \bullet \ \bullet \\ \bullet \ \bullet \mid \bullet \ \bullet \mid \bullet \ \bullet \mid \bullet \ \bullet \mid \bullet \ \bullet \end{array}\right\} \ 30 = 15 \times 2.$$

Into threes:

$$\left.\begin{array}{l} \bullet \ \bullet \ \bullet \mid \bullet \ \bullet \ \bullet \mid \bullet \ \bullet \ \bullet \mid \bullet \\ \bullet \ \bullet \mid \bullet \ \bullet \ \bullet \mid \bullet \ \bullet \ \bullet \mid \bullet \ \bullet \\ \bullet \mid \bullet \ \bullet \ \bullet \mid \bullet \ \bullet \ \bullet \mid \bullet \ \bullet \ \bullet \end{array}\right\} \ 30 = 10 \times 3.$$

Oral :

$$30 = 29 + 1, 28 + 2, 27 + 3, \text{ etc.}$$

30 is 30-fold of 1	1 is $\frac{1}{30}$ of 30
15-fold of 2	2 is $\frac{1}{15}$ of 30
10-fold of 3	3 is $\frac{1}{10}$ of 30
6-fold of 5	5 is $\frac{1}{6}$ of 30
5-fold of 6	6 is $\frac{1}{5}$ of 30
3-fold of 10	10 is $\frac{1}{3}$ of 30
2-fold of 15	15 is $\frac{1}{2}$ of 30

Of what equal numbers does 30 consist ?
Of what 2, 3, 4, 5, 6 unequal numbers ?

Rapid Work.

$30 + 15 + 3 \times 5 + 5 + 10$?
$(3 \times 5) + (2 \times 4) + 7 + 10 \times 3$?
4×6, the half, again the half, $\times 5$?

Combining.

$30 - 19$.
$(19 = 10 + 9, 30 - 10 = 20, 20 - 9 = 11, 30 - 19 = 11.)$
How do you get the double of 15 ?
$(15 = 1$ ten and 5 units ; 2×1 ten $= 2$ tens ; 2×5 units $= 10$ units $= 1$ ten ; 2 tens $+ 1$ ten $= 3$ tens $= 30$.)
Compare 30 with 16.
$(30 = 3$ tens ; $16 = 1$ ten $+ 6$ units. I must add to the 6 units 4 units to complete the second ten, and still 1 ten to get 3 tens. Therefore 30 has 1 ten $+ 4$ units $= 14$ more than 16, and 16 is 1 ten $+ 4$ units, or 14 less than 30.) *
$10 \times 3 = 6$ times what number ?
If I take 3×5 from a number, I get 5×3 as remainder. What is the number ?

---

* This method of adding and subtracting is universally practised at present in the German schools, with most excellent results. The tens are the stepping-stones of the method.

II.—The Applied Number.

In 30 days how many weeks? How many dozen? How many score?

If it costs me 2 dollars a day when I travel, how many days can I travel and spend 30 dollars?

A dollar contains 10 dimes. How many dollars in 30 dimes?

A workman received 6 dollars a week. How much will he receive in 5 weeks?

A piece of linen was 10 yards long. How many feet long was it?

Charles had a cane 2 feet 6 inches long. How many inches long was it?

William had 7 gallons and 2 quarts of water in a tub. How many quarts did he have?

If a shirt require 3 yards of cloth, how many shirts can be made from a piece containing 30 yards?

A golden eagle equals 10 dollars. If Joseph had 3 eagles, how many dollars had he?

Mr. A. sold 3 sheep at 5 dollars each, and 4 pigs at 3 dollars each. How much did he lack of getting 30 dollars?

Five francs make 1 dollar. How many dollars are equal to 30 francs?

A teacher divided 30 apples among his pupils, giving the boys half and the girls half. The boys received each 3 apples, and the girls each 5. How many pupils had he?

FIFTIETH STEP.

THE FIFTY.

$5 \times 10 = 50$

How many ones stand perpendicularly under each other?

Write these fives in horizontal lines.

Write 50 in twos. How many stand in a line?

(Continue as in preceding numbers.)

Oral and Written.

$50 = 50 \times 1$	$50 \div 1 = 50$
25×2	$2 = 25$
16×3 (2)	$3 = 16$ (2)
12×4 (2)	$4 = 12$ (2)
10×5	$5 = 10$
8×6 (2)	$6 = 8$ (2)
7×7 (1)	$7 = 7$ (1)
6×8 (2)	$8 = 6$ (2)
5×9 (5)	$9 = 5$ (5)
5×10	$10 = 5$

Rapid Work.

$50 \div 2 \div 5 \times 6 - 15 + 3$?

$10 \times 5 - 10 - 10 - 10 - 10 - 5$?

$25 \times 2 \div 5 + 15 - 5 + 20 + 10$?

$30 \div 2 \times 3 + 5 + 5 + 40 \div 50$?

$50 - 2 - 4 - 4 + 4 + 5 \times 3 - 15$?

Combining.

The nfth part of 50 is double what number?

The half of 50 is 5 times what number?

How does $\frac{1}{5}$ of 50 compare with $\frac{1}{5}$ of 25?

$\frac{1}{5}$ of $25 = \frac{1}{10}$ of what number?

II.—The Applied Number.

How many weeks in 50 days?

How many pounds avoirdupois in 50 ounces?

If I have 50 cents, how many 10-cent pieces does it equal? How many 5-cent pieces?

In 50 inches how many feet?

Charles receives from his aunt a 25-cent piece; from his father he received another. How many cents did he get?

A milkman shipped to New York 5 cans of milk, each containing 10 gallons. How many gallons did he ship?

Mary buys 50 cents' worth of muslin, paying 10 cents a yard. How many yards does she get?

A coal-dealer invested 50 dollars in coal at 4 dollars a ton. How many tons did he buy?

HUNDREDTH STEP.

(*The Last Step of the First Course.*)

THE HUNDRED.

The counting upwards and downwards with numbers from 1 to 10, beginning with both 1 and 2, must be done without hesitation, rapidly and accurately. In counting in concert, the teacher should frequently stop the pupils with questions as before. To illustrate :

Counting with 2, beginning with 1 : 1, 3, 5, 7, 9, 11, 13, (Stop! In what ten are we? How many units does it lack of being complete? How many tens still remain to complete 100? How many units?) 15, 17, 19, 21, etc.

Counting with 6, beginning with 2 : 2, 8, 14, 20, 26, 32, (Stop! In what ten are we? How many units are lacking to complete the ten? How many tens to complete 100?) 38, 44, 50, etc.

Counting with 6, beginning with 99 : 99, 93, 87, 81, (Stop! Ask questions as above.)

(Count both upwards and downwards with all numbers from 1 to 10 in this manner. This will be found a most valuable exercise. If the drill has been faithfully kept up with all preceding numbers, it will now be very easy and satisfactory.)

Written.

Pupils should write the above tables as follows:

1 + 2 = 3	or 1 + 7 = 8	or 100 − 8 = 92
3 + 2 = 5	8 + 7 = 15	92 − 8 = 84
5 + 2 = 7	15 + 7 = 22	84 − 8 = 76
7 + 2 = 9	22 + 7 = 29	etc.
etc.	etc.	

10 × 10 = 100

100 = 100 × 1	100 ÷ 1 = 100
50 × 2	2 = 50
33 × 3 (1)	3 = 33 (1)
25 × 4	4 = 25
20 × 5	5 = 20
16 × 6 (4)	6 = 16 (4)
14 × 7 (2)	7 = 14 (2)
12 × 8 (4)	8 = 12 (4)
11 × 9 (1)	9 = 11 (1)
10 × 10	10 = 10

100 = 99 + 1, 98 + 2, 97 + 3, etc.

100 is 100-fold of 1	1 is $\frac{1}{100}$ of 100
50-fold of 2	2 is $\frac{1}{50}$
25-fold of 4	4 is $\frac{1}{25}$
20-fold of 5	5 is $\frac{1}{20}$
5-fold of 20	20 is $\frac{1}{5}$
2-fold of 50	50 is $\frac{1}{2}$

Rapid Work.

$$100 \div 2 + 10 \div 30 \times 25 \times 2 ?$$
$$4 \times 25 - 50 \div 5 \times 10 - 75 \times 3 + 25 ?$$

All possible combinations in multiplication have already been learned in the course of the various exercises, but may now be arranged in the multiplication table and practised.

1	2	3	4	5	6	7	8	9	10
2	4	6	8	10	12	14	16	18	20
3	6	9	12	15	18	21	24	27	30
4	8	12	16	20	24	28	32	36	40
5	10	15	20	25	30	35	40	45	50
6	12	18	24	30	36	42	48	54	60
7	14	21	28	35	42	49	56	63	70
8	16	24	32	40	48	56	64	72	80
9	18	27	36	45	54	63	72	81	90
10	20	30	40	50	60	70	80	90	100

$2 \times 2 = 4$								
$2 \times 3 = 6$	$3 \times 3 = 9$							
$2 \times 4 = 8$	$3 \times 4 = 12$	$4 \times 4 = 16$						
$2 \times 5 = 10$	$3 \times 5 = 15$	$4 \times 5 = 20$	$5 \times 5 = 25$					
$2 \times 6 = 12$	$3 \times 6 = 18$	$4 \times 6 = 24$	$5 \times 6 = 30$	$6 \times 6 = 36$				
$2 \times 7 = 14$	$3 \times 7 = 21$	$4 \times 7 = 28$	$5 \times 7 = 35$	$6 \times 7 = 42$	$7 \times 7 = 49$			
$2 \times 8 = 16$	$3 \times 8 = 24$	$4 \times 8 = 32$	$5 \times 8 = 40$	$6 \times 8 = 48$	$7 \times 8 = 56$	$8 \times 8 = 64$		
$2 \times 9 = 18$	$3 \times 9 = 27$	$4 \times 9 = 36$	$5 \times 9 = 45$	$6 \times 9 = 54$	$7 \times 9 = 63$	$8 \times 9 = 72$	$9 \times 9 = 81$	
$2 \times 10 = 20$	$3 \times 10 = 30$	$4 \times 10 = 40$	$5 \times 10 = 50$	$6 \times 10 = 60$	$7 \times 10 = 70$	$8 \times 10 = 80$	$9 \times 10 = 90$	$10 \times 10 = 100$

The multiplication table can also be written in rows as follows :

$$2 \times 1 = 2; \; 2 \times 2 = 4; \; 2 \times 3 = 6, \text{ etc.};$$
$$3 \times 1 = 3; \; 3 \times 2 = 6; \; 3 \times 3 = 9, \text{ etc.};$$
$$4 \times 1 = 4; \; 4 \times 2 = 8; \; 4 \times 3 = 12, \text{ etc.};$$

and so forth until

$$10 \times 1 = 10; \; 10 \times 2 = 20; \; 10 \times 3 = 30, \text{ etc.}$$

The pupil must learn that the product is the same when the factors are alike, no matter in what order taken.

$$7 \times 6 = 42, \; 6 \times 7 = 42.$$

Besides what has already been given, the four fundamental rules must be practised with numbers above 10 until the pupils are brought to complete mastery of them, and are able to make various combinations with great rapidity and accuracy. A few examples follow which must be worked only orally :

a. (Addition)—

$$14 + 13 + 12 + 11$$
$$15 + 17 + 19 + 18$$
$$25 + 37 + 39 + 17$$
$$42 + 15 + 26 + 37$$
etc.

(The method of working is as follows: $42 + 10 = 52$, $52 + 5 = 57$, $57 + 20 = 77$, $77 + 6 = 83$, $83 + 30 = 113$, $113 + 7 = 120$.)

b. (Subtraction)—

$$90 - 19 - 12 - 11$$
$$98 - 32 - 41 - 24$$
$$90 - 16 - 17 - 28 - 29$$
$$97 - 12 - 34 - 16 - 27$$
etc.

(To be worked as follows: $97 - 10 = 87$, $87 - 2 = 85$, $85 - 30 = 55$, $55 - 4 = 51$, $51 - 10 = 41$, $41 - 6 = 35$, $35 - 20 = 15$, $15 - 7 = 8$.)

c. (Multiplication)—

$$3 \times 30, \quad 4 \times 22, \quad 2 \times 44, \quad 2 \times 27,$$
$$3 \times 25, \quad 4 \times 18, \quad 12 \times 5, \quad 33 \times 2,$$
$$35 \times 2, \quad 45 \times 3, \quad 15 \times 7, \quad 19 \times 4,$$
$$42 \times 6, \quad 17 \times 9,$$
etc.

(Employ the following method of solution: (17×9) $10 \times 9 = 90$, $7 \times 9 = 63$; $90 + 60 = 150$, $150 + 3 = 153$. (Likewise 15×37) $10 \times 37 = 370$, $5 \times 30 = 150$, $5 \times 7 = 35$; $370 + 100 = 470$, $470 + 50 = 520$, $520 + 35 = 555$.)

d. (Division)—

$$60 \div 3, \quad 69 \div 3, \quad 96 \div 4, \quad 72 \div 4,$$
$$84 \div 4, \quad 84 \div 12, \quad 68 \div 13, \quad 72 \div 18,$$
$$53 \div 4, \quad 62 \div 5, \quad 72 \div 3.$$

(Method as follows: $72 \div 3$ is $60 \div 3 = 20$ and $12 \div 3 = 4$. Thus $72 [60 + 12] \div 3 = 24 [20 + 4]$.

Another: $84 \div 12$ is $60 \div 12 = 5$ and $24 \div 12 = 2$. Thus $84 [60 + 24] \div 12 = 7 [5 + 2]$.

Another: $40 \div 18$ is $36 \div 18 = 2$. Thus $40 \div 18 = 2 (4)$.)

Combining.

The teacher will write a row of figures on the board to be added, subtracted, multiplied, and divided, placing the signs between. He then points to the exercises, and the pupils solve them rapidly. The teacher must always solve the examples himself. This holds good for all work in arithmetic, and is very important.

Such examples as the following must be rapidly worked by the pupils:

$$(3 \times 29) - (4 \times 16) + 7 \div 10 \times 9 \times 3?$$
$$(15 \times 6) - (45 \div 9) \times 37?$$
$$(4 \times 20) - 15 - 5 \div 20 \times 45?$$
$$90 - 45 - 5 \times 2 + 20 \div 10 + 6 \times 6?$$

As a test whether every number is comprehended by the pupil, let him name the factors of numbers from 1 to 100 without naming the numbers. Prime numbers can only be measured with 1. For example: 1×1, 2×1, 3×1, 2×2, 5×1, 2×3, 7×1, 2×4, or $2 \times 2 \times 2$, 3×3, etc.

It is important that the children know readily that 52 = 4 × 13, 68 = 4 × 17, 95 = 5 × 19, and so on to 100.

Such exercises as the following should be thoroughly drilled:

2 × 11 = 22	2 × 12 = 24	2 × 13 = 26
3 × 11 = 33	3 × 12 = 36	3 × 13 = 39
4 × 11 = 44	4 × 12 = 48	4 × 13 = 52
5 × 11 = 55	5 × 12 = 60	5 × 13 = 65
etc.	etc.	etc.

2 × 14 = 28
3 × 14 = 42, and so on till 5 × 19 = 95.

The prime and composite numbers can be arranged as follows:

1 prime number
2 " "
3 " "
4 = 2 × 2
5 prime number
6 = 2 × 3
7 prime number
8 = 2 × 2 × 2
9 = 3 × 3
10 = 2 × 5
11 prime number
12 = 2 × 2 × 3
13 prime number
14 = 2 × 7
15 = 3 × 5
16 = 2 × 2 × 2 × 2
17 prime number
18 = 3 × 3 × 2

and so forth till 100. This must be thoroughly drilled.

Combining.

A man gave away $\frac{1}{4}$ of 100 dollars, and then $\frac{1}{3}$ of the rest. What part of the whole amount had he still?

I have taken a number 3 times and obtained 4 more than $\frac{1}{3}$ of 100. What was the number?

5 times what number is 5 less than 100?

(The number which is 5 less than 100 is 95. If 95 is 5 times a number, that number is contained 5 times in 95. $\frac{1}{5}$ of 95 = 19.)

75 is 3 times $\frac{1}{4}$ of what number?
50 is $\frac{1}{8}$ of 4 times what number?
60 is 6 times $\frac{1}{10}$ of what number?

II.—The Applied Number.

100 cents = how many dimes? quarters? halves?
100 feet = how many yards?
100 days = how many months (of 30 days)?
100 months = how many years?
100 quarts = how many gallons?
100 pints = how many quarts?
100 things = how many dozen? score?
100 ounces = how many pounds?
100 days = how many weeks?

Charles received 4 quarters as a birthday present. He spent 50 cents for fruit and nuts, gave 20 cents away, and lost 10 cents. How much had he left?

How many days in 100 hours?

How many hours in 100 minutes?

A farmer had 100 pecks of clover seed. How many bushels had he?

Mary had a cord 100 inches long. How many feet is that?

Mrs. A. took 8 dozen eggs to the store. How many eggs did she take?

My grandfather is fourscore and four years old. How many years is that?

January has 31 days, February 28, and March 31. How many days do they lack of 100?

Mr. Thomas sold 4 cows at $25 each, and laid out the money in sheep at $5 a head. How many sheep did he buy?

How many years in $\frac{1}{2}$ a century? $\frac{1}{4}$? $\frac{1}{10}$?

If a train of cars goes 20 miles an hour, how long will it take to go 100 miles?

A ship sailed 2 leagues an hour. How long did it take her to sail 96 miles?

If I saw a board 100 inches long in 4 equal pieces, how long will each piece be?

(Examples of this kind should be made by both teacher and pupils until the pupils are able to thoroughly apply the number 100.)

(This completes the work of the first two years according to Grube. Later educators in Germany accept the first year's work, but modify the second very materially. We append herewith a method which meets with very general favor in Germany. The two methods must not be mixed, and no attempt should be made to combine them. Accept one, reject the other.)

APPENDIX TO THE SECOND YEAR'S WORK.

The decimal system is the basis of all arithmetical operations after the 10 (the first year's work). The children should be introduced to this system the second year. They must not longer consider each number as an individual, but as a part of a system. Accordingly, the following should be the plan of procedure.

SECTION I.

Development of the numbers from 10–100 in the pure tens, and practice of the four fundamental operations within this range.

FIRST UNITY.
(Addition and Subtraction.)

First Step.

a.
$1 + 2 = 3$ $10 - 2 = 8$
$3 + 2 = 5$ $8 - 2 = 6$
$5 + 2 = 7$ $6 - 2 = 4$
$7 + 2 = 9$ $4 - 2 = 2$

$$1 + 3 = 4 \qquad\qquad 10 - 3 = 7$$
$$4 + 3 = 7 \qquad\qquad 7 - 3 = 4$$
$$7 + 3 = 10 \qquad\qquad 4 - 3 = 1$$

The same with 4 and 5.

b. We wish to count 100 miles. Children count 10 on the numeral frame. That we will call 10 miles. Again 10 miles must be counted.

$$10 \text{ miles} + 10 \text{ miles} = 20 \text{ miles}.$$

We must count very much farther before we get 100 miles. Count another 10 on the frame:

$$20 \text{ miles} + 10 \text{ miles} = 30 \text{ miles}.$$

Continue in this way until we get

$$90 \text{ miles} + 10 \text{ miles} = 100 \text{ miles}.$$

In the same manner reverse the process, commencing at 100 and subtracting 10 each time:

10 m. + 10 m. = 20 m.		100 m. — 10 m. = 90 m.
20 " + 10 " = 30 "		90 " — 10 " = 80 "
30 " + 10 " = 40 "		80 " — 10 " = 70 "
40 " + 10 " = 50 "		70 " — 10 " = 60 "
till		till
90 m. + 10 m. = 100 m.		20 m. — 10 m. = 10 m.

c. Run rapidly through the tens forwards and backwards, using the numeral frame or fingers:

10	100
20	90
30	80
40	70
till	till
100	10

d. With the frame develop the ordinals.

(Children say as the teacher indicates.)

That is the first 10 miles;
" second 10 "
" third 10 "

till

That is the tenth 10 miles.

Or,

That is the tenth   10 miles ;
    "   ninth   10   "
         etc.

e. Writing the tens forwards and backwards from dictation:

10	100
20	90
30	80
etc.	etc.

Second Step.

a. Oral practice in intervals of 20, 30, 40, forwards and backwards:

$20 + 20 = 40$	$100 - 20 = 80$
$40 + 20 = 60$	$80 - 20 = 60$
$60 + 20 = 80$	$60 - 20 = 40$
$80 + 20 = 100$	$40 - 20 = 20$
$10 + 20 = 30$	$90 - 20 = 70$
$30 + 20 = 50$	$70 - 20 = 50$
$50 + 20 = 70$	$50 - 20 = 30$
$70 + 20 = 90$	$30 - 20 = 10$
$20 + 30 = 50$	$80 - 30 = 50$
$50 + 30 = 80$	$50 - 30 = 20$
$10 + 30 = 40$	$100 - 30 = 70$
$40 + 30 = 70$	$70 - 30 = 40$
$70 + 30 = 100$	$40 - 30 = 10$

In this same manner with the other numbers.

b. Practise writing from dictation after each group.

c. Exercises like the following:

$1 + 2 = 3$	$10 - 2 = 8$
$10 + 20 = 30$	$100 - 20 = 80$
$2 + 3 = 5$	$7 - 4 = 3$
$20 + 30 = 50$	$70 - 40 = 30$
$4 + 3 = 7$	$8 - 5 = 3$
$40 + 30 = 70$	$80 - 50 = 30$

d. Concrete examples:
A man travelled 30 miles, and afterwards 20 miles more.
How far did he go?

John had 70 miles to go. After he had gone 40 miles,
how much farther had he still to go?

(Other examples of this kind.)

Third Step.

The pupils have now learned that the tens progress the
same as the units, that they can be added and subtracted
the same as the units, and they have also learned how to
write the tens.

Fourth Step.

a.   10 miles + 20 miles + 30 miles = ?
     30 " + 40 " + 20 " = ?
     50 " + 30 " + 20 " = ?
        etc.

b.   90 miles — 30 miles — 20 miles = ?
     100 " — 40 " — 30 " = ?
     80 " — 10 " — 50 " = ?
        etc.

c.   30 + 40 — 50 + 10 — 20 = ?
     70 — 30 — 20 + 60 + 10 = ?
     60 + 40 — 50 — 30 + 40 = ?
        etc.

d. 40 = 10 + 30   40 = 60 — 20
    40 = 20 + 20   40 = 50 — 10
    50 = 10 + 40   50 = 80 — 30
    50 = 20 + 30   50 = 90 — 40
    60 = 10 + 50   30 = 70 — 40
    60 = 20 + 40   30 = 90 — 60
    60 = 30 + 30   60 = 100 — 40
        etc.

$$e. \quad 60 = 20 + 20 + \,?$$
$$70 = 10 + 30 + \,?$$
$$50 = 30 + 10 + \,?$$
$$80 = 40 + 10 + \,?$$
$$90 = 70 + 30 - \,?$$
$$60 = 80 + 10 - \,?$$
$$40 = 50 + 20 - \,?$$

Each group to be written from dictation.

f. Concrete examples :

If a man travels 20 and 30 and 40 miles, how far has he gone ?

From A to B is 30 miles, from B to C is 50 miles, from C to D is 20 miles.   How far is A from D ?

If I had 90 miles to travel, and have already gone 30 miles, how many miles remain to travel ?

(Make more examples of this kind.)

SECOND UNITY.
(Multiplication and Division.)
First Step.

Review first a few numbers :

1 × 1 = 1	1 in 1 = 1
2 × 1 = 2	1 in 2 = 2
3 × 1 = 3	1 in 3 = 3
4 × 1 = 4	1 in 4 = 4
till	till
10 × 1 = 10	1 in 10 = 10

Second Step.

a. Count off the first 10 miles on the numeral frame, also the 2d, 3d, etc., till the 10th.

b. Name the ordinals forwards and backwards from the frame as follows :

That is the first   10 miles ;
      "   second 10   "

till

That is the tenth   10 miles.

Also,

That is the tenth 10 miles;
"   ninth 10 "
etc.

c.   1 × 10 miles = 10 miles;
    2 × 10 "   = 20 "
    3 × 10 "   = 30 "
    4 × 10 "   = 40 "
             till
   10 × 10 miles = 100 miles.

The same backwards.
d. Then briefly:

1 × 10 = 10	10 × 10 = 100
2 × 10 = 20	9 × 10 = 90
3 × 10 = 30	8 × 10 = 80
4 × 10 = 40	7 × 10 = 70
till	till
10 × 10 = 100	1 × 10 = 10

Third Step.

a. Practise with concrete and abstract numbers, oral and written, without the numeral frame:

10 miles in 10 miles once;
10 "   20 "   twice; $10 = \frac{1}{2}$ of 20
10 "   30 "   3 times; $10 = \frac{1}{3}$ of 30
till
10 "   100 "   10 times. $10 = \frac{1}{10}$ of 100, etc.

b. Multiplications and divisions of abstract and concrete numbers not following regular order:
If a boy walks 10 miles a day, how far will he go in 2 days? In 3, 5, 7, 6, 9, 8, 10?
How much is $\frac{1}{2}$ of 20 miles? $\frac{1}{3}$ of 30 miles? $\frac{2}{3}$ of 30 miles? $\frac{1}{5}$ of 50 miles? $\frac{2}{5}$ of 50 miles? etc.

Fourth Step.

Writing and reading of tens in both the form of multiplication and division.

Fifth Step.

GENERAL APPLICATION.

$70 \div 10 = ?$ $60 \div 10 = ?$ $40 \div 10 = ?$
How many times 10 in 30? 90? 50? 100?
$(6 \times 10) + (4 \times 10) = ?$
$(7 \times 10) - (5 \times 10) = ?$
4×10 miles are how many more than 2×10 miles?
How many less than 7×10 miles?
How much is $\frac{1}{2}$ of 20? $\frac{2}{3}$ of 30? $\frac{1}{4}$ of 40? $\frac{2}{5}$ of 50?
How much is $\frac{1}{2}$ of 20 + $\frac{1}{3}$ of 30 + $\frac{2}{3}$ of 30?
How much is $\frac{2}{5}$ of 50 - $\frac{2}{3}$ of 30?
What number is 3×10 more than 5×10?
A man has 70 miles to travel. How long will it take him if he travels 10 miles a day?
How many miles has he still to go after he has travelled 4 days?
If a boy earns 10 cents a day for 7 days, how much does he lack of 1 dollar?

SECTION II.

Development of the whole range from 1 to 100 with all numbers between as sums of tens and units, in sections from 1 to 20, 20 to 30, 30 to 40, 40 to 50, 50 to 60, 60 to 80, 80 to 100. This includes addition and subtraction within these limits.

THIRD UNITY. 1 to 20.

(Addition and Subtraction of Pure Units and Tens. 10 + 6; 20 − 5.)

First Step.

Count the numbers from 1 to 20 on the frame forwards and backwards. Write the numbers 11 to 20.
Children should be taught—
1. To distinguish tens and units.
2. Different values of figures according to the position or order in which they are found.
3. That the units progress just the same in connection with the tens as when alone.

Second Step.

10 years + 1 year = 11 years ;
10 " + 2 years = 12 "
10 " + 3 " = 13 "
till
10 years + 10 years = 20 years.

20 years — 10 years = 10 years ;
19 " — 9 " = 10 "
18 " — 8 " = 10 "
till
11 years — 1 year = 10 years.

1 ten + 1 unit = 11
1 " + 2 units = 12
1 " + 3 " = 13
till
1 ten + 10 units = 20

11 = 1 ten + 1 unit.
12 = 1 " + 2 units.
13 = 1 " + 3 units, etc.

10 + 1 = 11	20 — 1 = 19
10 + 2 = 12	20 — 2 = 18
10 + 3 = 13	20 — 3 = 17
till	till
10 + 10 = 20	20 — 10 = 10

Dictate the following for the pupils to write rapidly :
14, 11. 17, 13, 19, 12, etc.
The number consisting of 1 ten and 5 units, 1 ten and 7 units, 1 ten and 6 units, etc.
A child is 10 years old. How old will he be in 3 years? In 5, 6, 9, 7, 2?
(Other practical questions.)

Third Step.

Separating the numbers from 11 to 20 into tens and units, as well as forming these numbers from this and units. This must be oral and written.

15 = 1 ten + 5 units.
18 = 1 ten + 8 units.

1 ten + 9 units = 19, etc.

FOURTH UNITY. 1 to 30.

(Addition and Subtraction of Pure Tens in connection with Mixed Tens: 14 + 10; 28 - 10.

First Step.

Count the numbers from 20 to 30 forwards and backwards on the frame. Write the same.

Separate into tens and units. Form the new numbers from tens and units.

Second Step.

a. Review the former exercises oral and written, and extend them.

20 miles + 1 mile = 21 miles;
20 " + 2 miles = 22 "
20 " + 3 " = 23 "
etc.

30 miles — 1 mile = 29 miles;
30 " — 2 miles = 28 "
30 " — 3 " = 27 "
etc.

b. 10 miles + 1 mile = 11 miles;
20 " + 1 " = 21 "
10 " + 2 miles = 12 "
20 " + 2 " = 22 "
10 " + 3 " = 13 "
20 " + 3 " = 23 "
etc.

10 miles — 1 mile = 9 miles;
20 " — 1 " = 19 "
30 " — 1 " = 29 "
10 " — 2 miles = 8 "
20 " — 2 " = 18 "
30 " — 2 " = 28 "
etc.

Give also abstract numbers in irregular order:

1 + 10 = 11	11 + 10 = 21
2 + 10 = 12	12 + 10 = 22
3 + 10 = 13	13 + 10 = 23
2 + 10 = 12	21 − 10 = 11
12 − 10 = 2	22 − 10 = 12
13 − 10 = 3	23 − 10 = 13

etc.

Practise these exercises and others until the pupils are able to give all possible combinations below 30 in adding and subtracting.

Third Step.

a. Explain the numbers 12 and 21. (12 = 1 ten and 2 units; 21 = 2 tens and 1 unit.) Other numbers in the same manner.

b. 14 hours + 10 hours = 24 hours;
18   "   + 10   "   = 28   "
7   "   + 10   "   = 17   "
etc.

29 hours − 10 hours = 19 hours;
19   "   − 10   "   = 9   "
etc.

c. 7 + 3 + 5 + 10 =
20 − 8 + 10 − 20 =
26 − 20 + 10 + 10 =
15 + 10 − 20 + 25 =

FIFTH UNITY.

First Step.

a. Length of the schoolhouse · 30 paces (children know as far as that), and still 8 paces.
Width of the schoolhouse : 16 paces.
Other exercises that require counting.
b. Review the numbers 1 to 30.

Second Step.

a. Extend the counting to 40 : 30 paces + 8 paces, etc.

b. Count on the numeral frame from 30 to 40, 1 to 40, forwards and backwards.

c. Write the new numbers from dictation, and separate them into tens and units.

Third Step.

Exercises like the previous ones extended to 40.

a. $10 + 1 = 11$ $20 + 1 = 21$ $30 + 1 = 31$
$10 + 2 = 12$ $20 + 2 = 22$ $30 + 2 = 32$
etc.

$10 - 1 = 9$ $20 - 1 = 19$ $30 - 1 = 29$ $40 - 1 = 39$
$10 - 2 = 8$ $20 - 2 = 18$ $30 - 2 = 28$ $40 - 2 = 38$
etc.

b. $10 + 1$ $10 + 2$ $10 + 3$
$20 + 1$ $20 + 2$ $20 + 3$
$30 + 1$ $30 + 2$ $30 + 3$
etc.

$10 - 1$ $10 - 2$ $10 - 3$
$20 - 1$ $20 - 2$ $20 - 3$
$30 - 1$ $30 - 2$ $30 - 3$
etc.

c. $11 + 10$ $21 + 10$ $11 + 20$
$12 + 10$ $22 + 10$ $12 + 20$

$11 - 10$ $21 - 10$
$12 - 10$ $22 - 10$
etc.

d.   Mixed exercises :

$$10 + 11 + 10 =$$
$$20 + 11 - 1 + 10 =$$
$$40 - 11 + 6 =$$
$$40 - 21 + 6 =$$
$$30 - 22 + 10 = \text{ etc.}$$

Fourth Step.

a. Write 12, 21, 13, 31, 23, 32.
Separate into tens and units.

b. 24 paces + 10 paces — 20 paces =
20 years + 17 years + 2 years — 15 years =
  etc.

Continue until the new numbers are thoroughly mastered.

SIXTH UNITY. 1 to 50.
SEVENTH UNITY. 1 to 60.
EIGHTH UNITY. 1 to 80.
NINTH ·UNITY. 1 to 100.

The method pursued in these will be the same as previously given, and therefore needs no further explanation. Dollars and cents can be taught in the last "unity."

SECTION III.

Development of the whole range from 1 to 100 by building each number from products of small numbers. This includes multiplication and division within these limits.

TENTH UNITY.
(Multiplying and dividing by 2.)

First Step.

Children should be drilled in the kinds of coins from 1 dollar down, the coins being shown them. They should be able to tell quickly how many cents each coin equals in value. Attention must be called to the differences between the coins, so that the children can readily distinguish them. Little examples should be made, the children working them out with actual or toy money in their hands. Let the children make examples.

Second Step.

a. Count the cents which make 10 two-cent pieces. Count the same number on the numeral frame. The children arrange the balls on the frame in 10 twos perpendicularly under each other, and say as the teacher points :

That is the first two cents;
"   second   "
"   third   "
till
That is the tenth two cents.

b. Count 2 cents, 4 cents, 6 cents to 20 cents.
c. Give the exercises that follow :

That is 1×2 cents;
" 2×2 "
" 3×2 "
till
That is 10×2 cents.

d. 1×2 cents $= 2$ cents;
2×2 " $= 4$ "
3×2 " $= 6$ "
etc.

2 cents $= 1 \times 2$ cents;
4   " $= 2 \times 2$ "
6   " $= 3 \times 2$ "
etc.

e. Abstract :

$1 \times 2 = 2$	$2 = 1 \times 2$
$2 \times 2 = 4$	$4 = 2 \times 2$
$3 \times 2 = 6$	$6 = 3 \times 2$
till	till
$10 \times 2 = 20$	$20 = 10 \times 2$

Practise and write forwards and backwards.

Third Step.

Complete these numbers with abstract and concrete oral and written examples.

a. 1×2 cents $=\ \ 2$ cents;
3×2 " $= 6$ "
5×2 " $= 10$ "
7×2 " $= 14$ "
9×2 " $= 18$ "

$$4 \text{ cents} = 2 \times 2 \text{ cents};$$
$$8 \quad `` \quad = 4 \times 2 \quad ``$$
$$12 \quad `` \quad = 6 \times 2 \quad ``$$
$$16 \quad `` \quad = 8 \times 2 \quad ``$$
$$20 \quad `` \quad = 10 \times 2 \quad ``$$

b. 2 in 2 = once;
2 in 4 = twice;
2 in 6 = three times;
till
2 in 20 = ten times.

$\frac{1}{2}$ of 4 = 2	$2 = \frac{1}{2}$ of 4
$\frac{1}{3}$ of 6 = 2	$2 = \frac{1}{3}$ of 6
$\frac{1}{4}$ of 8 = 2	$2 = \frac{1}{4}$ of 8
till	till
$\frac{1}{10}$ of 20 = 2	$2 = \frac{1}{10}$ of 20

c. Concrete and abstract exercises in multiplying and dividing with 2 taken in irregular order.

Fourth Step.

a. An orange costs 2 cents. What will 4 oranges cost? 8? 10?

If you practise music 2 hours a day, how many hours will you practise in 4 days? In a week? In 10 days?

A boy steps 2 feet each time he steps; how many feet will he go in 7 steps? In 5? In 9?

(Other examples.)

b. 6 × 2 years + 2 × 2 years;
5 × 2 `` + 4 × 2 ``
4 × 2 `` + 3 × 2 ``
etc.

10 × 2 years − 3 × 2 years;
7 × 2 `` − 5 × 2 ``
8 × 2 `` − 2 × 2 ``
etc.

c. 4 × 2 hours + 15 hours =
9 × 2 `` + 12 ``
7 × 2 `` + 10 ``
etc.

$$8 \times 2 \text{ hours} - 10 \text{ hours};$$
$$10 \times 2 \quad \text{``} \quad - 16 \quad \text{``}$$
$$12 \times 2 \quad \text{``} \quad - 18 \quad \text{``}$$

etc.

d.

$10 = 1 \times 10$	$12 = 1 \times 10 + 2$	$14 = 1 \times 10 + 4$
$10 = 5 \times 2$	$12 = 6 \times 2$	$14 = 6 \times 2 + 2$
$11 = 1 \times 10 + 1$	$13 = 1 \times 10 + 3$	$15 = 1 \times 10 + 5$
$11 = 5 \times 2 + 1$	$13 = 6 \times 2 + 1$	$15 = 2 \times 6 + 3$

In the same manner to 20.

e.

$1 \times 2 \text{ tens} = 2 \text{ tens} = 20$	$1 \times 20 = 20$
$2 \times 2 \quad\text{``} \quad = 4 \quad\text{``} \quad = 40$	$2 \times 20 = 40$
$3 \times 2 \quad\text{``} \quad = 6 \quad\text{``} \quad = 60$	$3 \times 20 = 60$
$4 \times 2 \quad\text{``} \quad = 8 \quad\text{``} \quad = 80$	$4 \times 20 = 80$
$5 \times 2 \quad\text{``} \quad = 10 \quad\text{``} \quad = 100$	$5 \times 20 = 100$

20 in 20 = once.	20 is $\frac{1}{2}$ of 40
20 in 40 = twice.	20 is $\frac{1}{3}$ of 60
20 in 60 = 3 times.	20 is $\frac{1}{4}$ of 80
20 in 80 = 4 "	20 is $\frac{1}{5}$ of 100
20 in 100 = 5 "	

f.

$2 \times 11 = 22$	$\frac{1}{2}$ of $22 = 11$
$2 \times 12 = 24$	$\frac{1}{2}$ of $24 = 12$
$2 \times 21 = 42$	$\frac{1}{2}$ of $42 = 21$
$2 \times 22 = 44$	$\frac{1}{2}$ of $44 = 22$

(Other numbers in irregular order.)

ELEVENTH UNITY.

(Multiplication and Division by 3.)

First Step.

a. Count off threes on the numeral frame and arrange them perpendicularly under each other.

♪ Name them as follows, the teacher pointing as the pupil names:

That is the first 3;
" second 3;
" third 3;
till
That is the tenth 3.

b. Count in intervals of 3: 3, 6, 9, 12, 15, to 30, forwards and backwards.

c.
1 × 3 dollars = 3 dollars;	3 dollars = 1 × 3 dollars;
2 × 3 " = 6 "	6 " = 2 × 3 "
3 × 3 " = 9 "	9 " = 3 × 3 "
till	till

10 × 3 dollars = 30 dollars. 30 dollars = 10 × 3 dollars.

Practise forwards and backwards with concrete and abstract numbers.

Second and *Third Steps* by the same plan as previously given.

Fourth Step.

a.
$$1 \times 3 = 3 \qquad 1 \times 30 = 30$$
$$2 \times 3 = 6 \qquad 2 \times 30 = 60$$
$$3 \times 3 = 9 \qquad 3 \times 30 = 90$$

b.
3 × 1 = 3	3 × 11 = 33	3 × 21 = 63	3 × 31 = 93
3 × 2 = 6	3 × 12 = 36	3 × 22 = 66	3 × 32 = 96
3 × 3 = 9	3 × 13 = 39	3 × 23 = 69	3 × 33 = 99

c.
3 ÷ 3 = 1	33 ÷ 3 = 11	63 ÷ 3 = 21	93 ÷ 3 = 31
6 ÷ 3 = 2	36 ÷ 3 = 12	66 ÷ 3 = 22	96 ÷ 3 = 32
9 ÷ 3 = 3	39 ÷ 3 = 13	69 ÷ 3 = 23	99 ÷ 3 = 33

TWELFTH UNITY.
(Multiplication and Division by 4.)

Follow the same plan as before. In the last step introduce also:

a.
$$1 \times 4 = 4 \qquad 1 \times 40 = 40$$
$$2 \times 4 = 8 \qquad 2 \times 40 = 80$$
$$3 \times 4 = 12 \qquad 3 \times 40 = 120$$
$$4 \times 4 = 16 \qquad 4 \times 40 = 160$$

b.
4 × 1 = 4	4 × 11 = 44	4 × 21 = 84
4 × 2 = 8	4 × 12 = 48	4 × 22 = 88
4 × 3 = 12	4 × 13 = 52	4 × 23 = 92
4 × 4 = 16	4 × 14 = 56	4 × 24 = 96

$$4 \div 4 = 1 \qquad 44 \div 4 = 11 \qquad 84 \div 4 = 21$$
$$8 \div 4 = 2 \qquad 48 \div 4 = 12 \qquad 88 \div 4 = 22$$
$$12 \div 4 = 3 \qquad 52 \div 4 = 13 \qquad 92 \div 4 = 23$$
$$16 \div 4 = 4 \qquad 56 \div 4 = 14 \qquad 96 \div 4 = 24$$

THIRTEENTH UNITY.
(Multiplication and Division by 5.)

Add to the plan of the previous steps :

a.
$$1 \times 5 = 5 \qquad\qquad 1 \times 50 = 50$$
$$2 \times 5 = 10 \qquad\qquad 2 \times 50 = 100$$
$$3 \times 5 = 15 \qquad\qquad 3 \times 50 = 150$$
$$4 \times 5 = 20 \qquad\qquad 4 \times 50 = 200$$
$$5 \times 5 = 25 \qquad\qquad 5 \times 50 = 250$$

b.
$$5 \times 1 = 5 \qquad\qquad 5 + 11 = 55$$
$$5 \times 2 = 10 \qquad\qquad 5 \times 12 = 60$$
$$5 \times 3 = 15 \qquad\qquad 5 \times 13 = 65$$
$$5 \times 4 = 20 \qquad\qquad 5 + 14 = 70$$
$$5 \times 5 = 25 \qquad\qquad 5 + 15 = 75$$

c.
$$5 \div 5 = 1 \qquad\qquad 55 \div 5 = 11$$
$$10 \div 5 = 2 \qquad\qquad 60 \div 5 = 12$$
$$15 \div 5 = 3 \qquad\qquad 65 \div 5 = 13$$
$$20 \div 5 = 4 \qquad\qquad 70 \div 5 = 14$$
$$25 \div 5 = 5 \qquad\qquad 75 \div 5 = 15$$

FOURTEENTH UNITY.
(With the 6.)

FIFTEENTH UNITY.
(With the 7.)

SIXTEENTH UNITY.
(With the 8.)

SEVENTEENTH UNITY.
(With the 9.)

Nothing further need be given to illustrate this system. The remaining steps are carried out in the same manner as those which are given in full.

Second Course.

I.

NUMBERS ABOVE 100.

THE THIRD YEAR.

FIRST HALF OF THE YEAR.

100 to 1000.

1. As the numbers between 100 and 1000 are combinations of the numbers within the first hundred, the only purpose of this course is to reduce them to their elements.

2. Thereby the pupil comes into possession of the secret of all accurate and rapid mental work in arithmetic, namely, always to operate with the smallest possible numbers; hence he needs none of the so-called "arithmetical knack."

3. In order to lead to an allsided representation of the number, it is impossible to consider all of the fundamental rules at once as heretofore; this will receive wider attention in the second half of the year. Mental and written arithmetic are now united at every step.

4. As the necessity of isolating each number now disappears, and because the allsided penetration and comprehension of each number must take place, the material will be divided in two parts only:

A. The pure number: measuring, separating, comparing, and combining.

B. The applied Number.

The child is now sufficiently mature gradually to leave simple mechanical processes and make more use of the understanding and reason. He must, however, master the processes, so as to be able to give them rapidly and almost mechanically. This side of the work is not to be neglected. Illustrations should still be used where needed, but he will learn chiefly by analogy from smaller numbers.

A.—Allsided Contemplation of the Pure Number.

(First Quarter.)

First Step.

Measuring of the numbers by the units of the Decimal System, by units, tens, and hundreds.

* *a.* (Oral.)

Count upwards and downwards from 100 to 1000. 10 splints can be bound together, and that is 1 ten. Around 10 of these bundles (100) a wide ribbon may be tied; 10 of these bundles make 1000. In this way the pupil gains a comprehension of 1000. Solid blocks divided by lines into 10 and 100 units can also be used.

During the counting the pupils must often be stopped and questioned as to which hundred and which ten they are in: How many units and tens are lacking in the tens and hundreds respectingly, and in the hundreds how many are lacking from a thousand?

For example: The teacher gives 768. The pupil will explain:

768 = 7 hundreds, 6 tens, 8 units. It lacks 2 units of completing the 7th ten, then 3 tens of completing the 8th hundred, and finally 2 hundreds of completing 1000.

829 = 8 hundreds, 2 tens, 9 units. Complete the analysis of 829.

Analyze in the same way 999, 500, 463, 271, 604.

What number is composed of 3 hundreds, 6 tens, and 5 units?

How many units in 7 hundreds, 8 tens, and 9 units?

How many units in one thousand? Tens? Hundreds?

Of what does 669 consist?

$$(6 \times 100) + (6 \times 10) + (9 \times 1)$$

b. (Written.)

To make it easier for beginners in writing, use the following plan :

h.	t.	u.	
1	0	1	= 101
4	8	0	= 480
10	0	0	= 1000

Numbers must be dictated for the pupils to write. When written on the blackboard, the figures should be named and the numbers read, etc., in order to acquire perfect mastery of the subject.

Finally, analogous to the oral work, dictated numbers should be written out as follows :

$$615 = 6 \times 100 + 1 \times 10 + 5 \times 1$$
$$204 = 2 \times 100 + 0 \times 10 + 4 \times 1$$
$$390 = 3 \times 100 + 9 \times 10 + 0 \times 1$$
$$1000 = 10 \times 100 + 0 \times 10 + 0 \times 1$$

or

$$615 = 600 + 10 + 5$$
$$204 = 200 + 4$$
$$390 = 300 + 90$$
$$1000 = 1000$$

In the following steps we shall give only one form, which will answer for both oral and written work. Neither is to be omitted, but they must be united, the oral taking precedence in order of time. Follow the plan suggested in the First Step.

SECOND STEP.

The pure hundreds measured with hundreds.

Measuring, comparing, rapid work, combining, are to be the same as in the First Course. With the number 2 in the First Course we obtained the following scheme :

$$1 + 1 = 2$$
$$2 \times 1 = 2$$
$$2 - 1 = 1$$
$$2 + 1 = 2$$

Conformably to this the pupil now learns :

200.

$$100 + 100 = 200$$
$$2 \times 100 = 200$$

$$200 - 100 = 100$$
$$200 \div 100 = 2$$

What number is contained twice in 200?
Of what number is 200 the double?
Of what number is 100 the half?
What number must I double in order to get 200?

(Give many other examples, following the method employed in teaching the 2. See Second Step in the First Course.)

300.

$$100 + 100 + 100 = 300$$
$$3 \times 100 = 300$$
$$300 \div 100 = 3$$
$$200 + 100 = 300$$
$$300 - 100 = 200$$
$$300 - 200 = 100$$
$$300 \div 200 = 1, \text{ with remainder of 100.}$$

300 is 100 more than 200, 200 more than 100.
200 is 100 less than 300, 100 more than a hundred.
100 is 200 less than 300, 100 less than 200.
300 is 3 times 100.
100 is $\frac{1}{3}$ of 300.

Of what equal and what unequal numbers does 300 consist?
How much is $300 - 100 - 100 + 200$?

$$300 \div 3 - 100 + 200 + 100 \times 100?$$
$$300 - 200 + 100 + 100 \div 3 - 100?$$

From what number can you take away 2×100 and have 100 left?
$\frac{1}{3}$ of 300 is how much less than $\frac{1}{2}$ of 300?
Which is greater, $\frac{1}{3}$ of 300 or $\frac{1}{2}$ of 200?

400.

1. Measure with 100 :

$$100 + 100 + 100 + 100 = 400$$
$$4 \times 100 = 400$$
$$400 - 100 - 100 - 100 = 100$$
$$400 \div 100 = 4$$

2. Measure with 200 :

$$200 + 200 = 400$$
$$2 \times 200 = 400$$
$$400 - 200 = 200$$
$$400 \div 200 = 2$$

3. Measure with 300 :

$$300 + 100 = 400$$
$$100 + 300 = 400$$
$$1 \times 300 + 100 = 400$$
$$400 - 200 = 200$$
$$400 - 300 = 100$$
$$400 \div 300 = 1 \ (100)$$

400 is 100 more than 300
200 more than 200
300 more than 100

300 is 100 less than 400
100 more than 200
200 more than 100, etc.

THIRD STEP.

Mixed hundreds measured with mixed hundreds.

$$220 = 2 \times 110, \text{ also } 1 \times 220$$
$$440 = 4 \times 110, \text{ also } 2 \times 220$$
$$660 = 6 \times 110, \text{ also } 3 \times 220$$

$$880 = 8 \times 110, \text{ also } 4 \times 220, 2 \times 440$$
$$990 = 9 \times 110, \text{ also } 3 \times 330$$

How may 888, 999, be considered?

$$888 = 8 \times 111, \text{ also } 4 \times 222,\ 2 \times 444$$
$$999 = 9 \times 111, \text{ also } 3 \times 333$$

$999 \div 333 =$	$888 \div 222 =$
$999 \div 3 =$	$888 \div 4 =$
$999 \div 111 =$	$888 \div 8 =$
etc.	etc.

Of what number is 120 the $\frac{1}{4}$, $\frac{1}{5}$, $\frac{1}{6}$?
What is $\frac{1}{4}$ of 844?
Of what number is 844 fourfold?
What number can I take 4 times from 844?
What number is contained 4 times in 844?
$\frac{1}{2}$ of 844 is how much greater than $\frac{1}{4}$?
$\frac{1}{3}$ of 333 is $\frac{1}{6}$ of what number?
Of what number is $\frac{1}{3}$ of 333 the ninth? ($\frac{1}{3}$ of 333 = 111. 111 is $\frac{1}{9}$ of 9 times 111 = 999.)
Compare 365 with 244.

$$365 = 3 \text{ hundreds} + 6 \text{ tens} + 5 \text{ units};$$
$$244 = 2 \text{ hundreds} + 4 \text{ tens} + 4 \text{ units}.$$

3 hundreds − 2 hundreds = 1 hundred; 6 tens − 4 tens = 2 tens; 5 units − 4 units = 1 unit. Therefore 365 − 244 = 1 h. + 2 t. + 1 u. = 121, or 365 is 121 greater than 244, and 244 is 121 less than 365.

What is the difference between 743 and 120?

743 = 7 h. + 4 t. + 3 u.; 120 = 1 h. + 2 t. + 0 u.; 7 h. − 1 h. = 6 h. 4 t. − 2 t. = 2 t.; 3 u. − 0 u. = 3 u. Therefore 743 − 120 = 6 h. + 2 t. + 3 u. = 623.

What number = 743 + 221?

743 = 7 h. + 4 t. + 3 u.; 221 = 2 h. + 2 t. + 1 u.; 7 h. + 2 = 9 h.; 4 t. + 2 t. = 6 t.; 3 u. + 1 = 4 u. Therefore 743 + 221 = 9 h. + 6 t. + 4 u. or 964.

How much is 111 + 212 + 313?
How much is 112 + 113 + 114?
Subtract 322 and 124 from 659.

Continue these exercises until the subject is understood.

Fourth Step.

Measuring of hundreds with tens.

I.

a. The pure hundreds.
Since $100 = 10 \times 10$,

$$2 \times 100 \text{ or } 200 = 2 \times 10 \times 10 = 20 \times 10$$
$$3 \times 100 \text{ or } 300 = 3 \times 10 \times 10 = 30 \times 10$$
$$4 \times 100 \text{ or } 400 = 4 \times 10 \times 10 = 40 \times 10$$
$$10 \times 100 \text{ or } 1000 = 10 \times 10 \times 10 = 100 \times 10 = 1000.$$

b. Hundreds with tens.
Since $100 = 10 \times 10$,

$$110 = (10 \times 10) + (1 \times 10) = 11 \times 10$$
$$120 = (10 \times 10) + (2 \times 10) = 12 \times 10$$
$$130 = (10 \times 10) + (3 \times 10) = 13 \times 10$$
$$140 = (10 \times 10) + (4 \times 10) = 14 \times 10$$
$$150 = (10 \times 10) + (5 \times 10) = 15 \times 10$$
$$190 = (10 \times 10) + (9 \times 10) = 19 \times 10$$
$$240 = (20 \times 10) + (4 \times 10) = 24 \times 10$$
$$990 = (90 \times 10) + (9 \times 10) = 99 \times 10$$

c. Hundreds with tens.
Since $100 = 10 \times 10$,

$$101 = (10 \times 10) + 1$$
$$109 = (10 \times 10) + 9$$
$$906 = (90 \times 10) + 6$$
$$814 = (81 \times 10) + 4$$

How many tens in 500, 900, 1000?
What number = 53 tens?
What number = 9 units more than 53 tens?
How many times 10 is 660, 420, 870?
Of what number is 10 the 42d part? The 66th? The 84th? The 70th?
How many tens in 879?

II.

Comparison.

Compare 400 with 900.

(400 = 40 tens; 900 = 90 tens; 90 tens — 40 tens = 50 tens. Therefore 900 has 50 tens more than 400, and 400 has 50 tens less than 900.)

How many are 55 tens less than 600? Than 660? Than 990?

(As 600 = 60 tens, 55 tens are 5 tens, or 50 less than 600.)

Of what 4 equal tens does 880 consist?

(880 = 88 tens, and as 88 tens = 4 × 22 tens, 880 is composed of 4 × 22 tens.)

What is the sum of 800, 180 and 20?

(800 + 180 + 20 = 80 + 18 + 2 tens = 100 tens = 1000.)

What is the difference between 160 and 210?

(210 or 21 tens — 160 or 16 tens = 5 tens = 50.)

60 × 10 = how many times 100?

What number has 8 tens and 9 units more than 490?

(The number which has 8 tens and 9 units more than 490 must equal 490 + 8 tens + 9 units. 490 or 49 tens + 8 tens = 57 tens = 570. 570 + 9 = 579.)

I have taken a number 87 times, added 9 to it and obtain 879. What is the number?

(879 = 87 tens + 9 units. Therefore I must have taken ten 87 times.)

How many more tens has 73 × 10 than the double of 240?

How many times is $\frac{1}{100}$ of 1000 contained in 500?

(1000 = 100 tens; $\frac{1}{100}$ of 100 tens = 1 ten; 500 = 50 tens; 50 tens contains 1 ten 50 times.)

$\frac{1}{3}$ of 630 = $\frac{1}{4}$ of what number?

(630 = 63 tens; $\frac{1}{3}$ of 63 tens = 21 tens; 21 tens is $\frac{1}{4}$ of 4 × 21 tens = 84 tens = 840.)

$\frac{1}{68}$ of 680 + $\frac{1}{24}$ of 240 is how much less than 10 × 36?

(As 680 = 68 tens, $\frac{1}{68}$ of 680 = 1 ten; and $\frac{1}{24}$ of 240 = 1 ten; both together = 2 tens. 10 × 36 = 36 tens, and 36 tens — 2 tens = 34 tens.)

The factors must also be changed in these **exercises.**

$$110 = 11 \times 10 = 10 \times 11$$
$$220 = 22 \times 10 = 10 \times 22$$
$$680 = 68 \times 10 = 10 \times 68$$
$$990 = 99 \times 10 = 10 \times 99$$

Of what is 990 composed?
How can 130 be composed from 13?
280 from 28? 560 from 56?
What number must I take 10 times to get 670?
Of what number is 67 one tenth?
What is $\frac{1}{87}$ of 670?
How many times is 79 contained in 790?
What number can I take 10 times from 790?   What 79 times?
$79 \times 10 = 10$ times what number?

These exercises lead us naturally to the next step.

FIFTH STEP.

Measuring a number by its factors.

I.

a. The pure hundreds.

$$100 = 2 \times 50, 4 \times 25, 5 \times 20, 10 \times 10$$

Therefore,

$$
\begin{aligned}
200 = 2 \times\ &2 \times 50 =\ 4 \times 50 \\
&2 \times\ 4 \times 25 =\ 8 \times 25 \\
&2 \times\ 5 \times 20 = 10 \times 20 \\
&2 \times 10 \times 10 = 20 \times 10 \\
300 = 3 \times\ &2 \times 50 =\ 6 \times 50 \\
&3 \times\ 4 \times 25 = 12 \times 25 \\
&3 \times\ 5 \times 20 = 15 \times 20 \\
&3 \times 10 \times 10 = 30 \times 10 = 20 \times 15
\end{aligned}
$$

b. Hundreds with tens.

$220 = 10 \times 22$. As $10 = 2 \times 5$, $220 = 2 \times 5 \times 22 = 2 \times 110$; and as $22 = 2 \times 11$, $10 \times 2 \times 11 = 10 \times 22$; and as $10 = 5 \times 2$, $5 \times 2 \times 22 = 5 \times 44$.

$$960 = 10 \times 96.$$
$$10 \times 2 \times 48 = 20 \times 48 = 48 \times 20$$
$$10 \times 3 \times 32 = 30 \times 32 = 32 \times 30$$
$$10 \times 4 \times 24 = 40 \times 24 = 24 \times 40$$
$$10 \times 6 \times 16 = 60 \times 16 = 16 \times 60$$
$$10 \times 8 \times 12 = 80 \times 12 = 12 \times 80$$

Or leaving the second factor unchanged:

$$10 \times 96 = 2 \times 5 \times 96 = 2 \times 480$$
$$5 \times 2 \times 96 = 5 \times 192$$

c. Hundreds with tens and units.

$$426 = (10 \times 42) + 6 \text{ or } (4 \times 100) + 26$$
$$(10 \times 2 \times 21) + 6 \text{ or } (20 \times 21) + 6$$
$$(10 \times 3 \times 14) + 6 \text{ or } (30 \times 14) + 6 = (14 \times 30) + 6$$
$$(2 \times 5 \times 42) + 6 = (2 \times 210) + 6$$
$$(5 \times 2 \times 42) + 6 = (5 \times 84) + 6$$

$$896 = (8 \times 100) + (8 \times 12) = 8 \times 112$$
$$(8 \times 112) = 2 \times 4 \times 112 = 2 \times 448$$
$$4 \times 2 \times 112 = 4 \times 224$$
$$(10 \times 89) + 6 = (2 \times 5 \times 89) + 6 = (2 \times 445) + 6$$
$$(5 \times 2 \times 89) + 6 = (5 \times 178) + 6$$

$$489 = (10 \times 48) + 9$$
$$(2 \times 240) + 9$$
$$(5 \times 96) + 9$$

Or:

$$(10 \times 4 \times 12) + 9 = (40 \times 12) + 9 = (12 \times 40) + 9$$
$$(10 \times 3 \times 16) + 9 = (30 \times 16) + 9 = (16 \times 30) + 9$$
$$(10 \times 2 \times 24) + 9 = (20 \times 24) + 9$$

300 is composed of how many twos? Threes? Fives?
How do you find the 25th part of 300?
($\frac{1}{25}$ of 100 = 4, so $\frac{1}{25}$ of 300 = 3 × 4 = 12.)
How does 300 arise out of 15?
(As $300 = 10 \times 30$, and $30 = 2 \times 15$, $300 = 10 \times 2 \times 15$
$= 20 \times 15$. I have taken 15 twenty times and obtained
300. Or: as $300 = 2 \times 150$, and $150 = 10 \times 15$, $300 = 2$
$\times 10 \times 15 = 20 \times 15$.)
How many times must I take 44 to get 220?
($220 = 10 \times 22 = 5 \times 2 \times 22 = 5 \times 44$.)

What number must I take 5 times from 426 in order to have 6 remainder?

$(426 = 10 \times 42) + 6 = (5 \times 2 \times 42) + 6 = (5 \times 84) + 6.$ So I must subtract 84 five times from 426, and have 6 remainder.)

How many times is 24 contained in 489?

$(489 = [10 \times 48] + 9 = [10 \times 2 \times 24] + 9 = [20 \times 24] + 9.$ 24 in 489 20 times with 9 remainder.)

II.

Comparison.

What is the difference between 980 and 377?

(980 = 98 tens, and 377 = 37 tens and 7 units. 98 tens − 37 tens = 61 tens − 7 units = 60 tens + 3 units = 603. Or: $900 - 300 = 600$; $80 - 77 = 3$; $980 - 377 = 603$.)

The difference between 980 and 377 is 3 times what number?

(The difference between 980 and 377 is 603. 603 is 3 times $\frac{1}{3}$ of 603. $\frac{1}{3}$ of 600 = 200, $\frac{1}{3}$ of 3 = 1, 200 + 1 = 201. Therefore, etc.)

$\frac{1}{4}$ and $\frac{1}{3}$ of 480 taken together is how many less than twice 480?

By what number must I divide 365 to get 5?

(If I divide 365 by a number and get 5, that number is contained 5 times in 365, or is $\frac{1}{5}$ of 365. $\frac{1}{5}$ of 300 = 60; $\frac{1}{5}$ of 65 = 13; $60 + 13 = 73$. Therefore, etc.)

What is the difference between $\frac{1}{22}$ and $\frac{1}{30}$ of 660?

The sum of 326 and 418 is how much greater than the sum of their halves?

I take 4 units from a number, and then divide the remainder by 16, and obtain a quotient of 60. What is the number?

(The unknown number is $16 \times 60 + 4$. 60 = 6 tens; 16×6 tens = 96 tens = 960; $960 + 4 = 964$. Therefore, etc.)

What number is 10 more than the double of 5×99?

SIXTH STEP.

Reduction of numbers from 1 to 1000 to their elements.

It does not matter in what order the numbers are taken, the chief object being practice in rapidly and accurately separating the numbers into their elements. The pupil is now able to tell at a glance into what parts the number must be separated. The teacher should make the work partly oral and partly written.

360.

300 + 60	3 × 100 + 3 × 20
180 + 180	3 × 120
200 + 160	10 × 36
320 + 40	5 × 72
336 + 24	20 × 18 = 18 × 20
etc.	9 × 40 etc.

320 + 45, 2 × 150 + 65, 2 × 182 + 1, 7 × 50 + 15, 14 × 25 + 15, 18 × 20 + 5, etc.

These six steps complete the work of the first quarter. The work now changes from the *pure* to the *applied* number. At this point especial attention should be given to compound numbers, weights, measures, money, etc. This will employ the second quarter. The teacher must supply a great many more examples than are here given, as the "applied number" is of great importance.

B.—All-sided Contemplation of the Applied Number.

(Second Quarter.)

a. The tens.

10 cents	=	1 dime.
10 dimes	=	1 dollar.
10 dollars	=	1 eagle.
3 dimes	=	30 cents.
5 dimes	=	50 cents or $\frac{1}{2}$ dollar.
50 "	=	5 dollars or $\frac{1}{2}$ eagle.

1 dollar = 10 dimes.
2 dollars = 20 "
3 " = 30 "
5 " = 50 "
10 " = 100 "
100 cents = 10 "   or 1 dollar.
100 dollars = 1000 dimes.
900 dimes = 30 × 30 dimes.
870 " = 29 × 30 "
840 " = 28 × 30 "
810 " = 27 × 30 "
etc.

9, 11, 17, 28 dollars = how many dimes?

9 dollars, 4 dimes, 24 cents = how many cents?

314, 365, 720, 799 cents, how many dimes? How many dollars?

25 dimes + 9 dimes + 17 dimes + 15 dimes = how many dimes? How many dollars?

From 2 dollars and 6 dimes take 15 dimes. 17 dimes. 25 dimes.

Divide the class into two divisions and let the first division give 3 times, and the second division 4 times, the numbers as the teacher names them.

Teacher.	1st Division.	2d Division.
25 dimes.	75 dimes.	100 dimes.
9 "	27 "	36 "
15 "	45 "	60 "
17 "	51 "	68 "

Again, the first division can give 3 times the number given, and the other division add the results.

Teacher.	1st Division.		
19 dimes.	5 dollars and 70 cents.		
12 "	3 "	" 60 "	
22 "	6 "	" 60 "	
2d Division....15 "	" 90 "		

In long examples the results of multiplying can be written in order to get the total correctly.

```
14 dollars 9 dimes.
15    "      7   "
16    "      4   "
17    "      8   "
18    "      6   "
19    "      5   "
───        ─
102   "      9   "
```

This will be added as follows, the operations being mental, only the above being set down :

14 dollars 9 dimes + 15 dollars = 29 dollars 9 dimes, + 7 dimes = 30 dollars 6 dimes; 30 dollars 6 dimes + 16 dollars 4 dimes = 47 dollars; 47 dollars + 17 dollars 8 dimes = 64 dollars 8 dimes; 64 dollars 8 dimes + 18 dollars 6 dimes = 83 dollars 4 dimes; 83 dollars 4 dimes + 19 dollars 5 dimes = 102 dollars 9 dimes.

2. Reverse the process, subtracting 19 dollars 5 dimes from 102 dollars 9 dimes, and so on until the first number, 14 dollars 9 dimes, is reached.

3. Multiply each of these numbers by 2, 3, 4, 5, and add the products, and divide the sum by 2, 3, 4, 5, and see if the sum of the original numbers is obtained.

```
14 dollars 9 dimes × 3 = 44 dollars 7 dimes.
15    "     7    "       47    "    1   "
16    "     4    "       49    "    2   "
17    "     8    "       53    "    4   "
18    "     6    "       55    "    8   "
19    "     5    "       58    "    5   "
───       ─            ───       ─
102   "     9    "       308    "    7   "
```

3 in 308 dollars 7 dimes = 102 dollars 9 dimes.

b. Tens and units.

```
24 dimes   = how many cents ?
24 dozen   =  "    "   things ?
24 dollars =  "    "   dimes ?
```

Pupils must be drilled in tables from

$$12 \times 1 \text{ to } 24 \times 12,$$
$$15 \times 1 \text{ to } 15 \times 15,$$
$$16 \times 1 \text{ to } 16 \times 16,$$
$$24 \times 1 \text{ to } 24 \times 24.$$

One dollar	=	10	dimes	=	100 cents.
One half "	=	5	"	=	50 "
One fourth "	=	$2\frac{1}{2}$	"	=	25 "
One fifth "	=	2	"	=	20 "
One tenth "	=	1	"	=	10 "
One twentieth "	=	$\frac{1}{2}$	"	=	5 "
One fiftieth "	=	$\frac{1}{5}$	"	=	2 "
One hundredth "	=	$\frac{1}{10}$	"	=	1 cent.
100 cents	=	10	"	=	1 dollar.
50 "	=	5	"	=	$\frac{1}{2}$ "
20 "	=	$2\frac{1}{2}$	"	=	$\frac{1}{5}$ "
		etc.			

The English weights and measures cannot well be applied to the Grube system, as the scales, instead of being decimal, are varying. And yet, with their present knowledge of the numbers as high as 1000, and with the applications of compound numbers made in the First Course during the first two years, the pupils should be able to master the subject of compound numbers in connection with the above work during the second quarter.

II.

THE FOUR FUNDAMENTAL RULES IN ABSTRACT AND CONCRETE NUMBERS —UNLIMITED RANGE.

THE THIRD YEAR.

SECOND HALF OF THE YEAR.

The division of the work is as follows :
A.—With abstract numbers.

Written :
1. Numeration.
2. Addition.
3. Subtraction.
4. Multiplication.
5. Division.

B.—With concrete numbers.

Oral :
1. Numeration.
2. Addition.
3. Subtraction.
4. Multiplication.
5. Division.

Mental and written arithmetic must not be separated, as though they were different studies ; mental arithmetic is the foundation ; here the idea has its beginning ; on this the written statement depends.

It becomes necessary in large numbers, and where several numbers are involved, to write them down in figures, so that they can be seen by the eye. The written work may thus be considered as only an assistant to the mental work.

It must not be thought that in addition there shall be only adding, and in subtraction only subtracting; but, as in the preceding steps, all the operations must be united as far as may be. Many examples must be given. The exercises in "rapid work" must not be neglected, and emulation among the pupils must be aroused to secure rapid and accurate work.

Only the important points of each step will be given, the filling in with material being left to the skill and tact of the teacher.

A.—With Abstract Numbers.

FIRST STEP.

Numeration.

a. (Oral.) Thousands and millions. If we have the 10 hundreds we have a new unity—the thousand. We can combine thousands into tens of thousands; tens of thousands into hundreds of thousands, etc., exactly as we combined units into tens, tens into hundreds, etc.

$$1 \times 1 \text{ unit} = 1 \text{ unit} = 1.$$
$$10 \times 1 \text{ unit} = 10 \text{ units} = 10.$$
$$10 \times 1 \text{ ten} = 10 \text{ tens} = 100.$$
$$10 \times 1 \text{ hundred} = 10 \text{ hundred} = 1 \text{ thous.} = 1000.$$
$$10 \times 1 \text{ thousand} = 10 \text{ thousand} = 1 \text{ tenth.} = 10000.$$
$$10 \times 1 \text{ ten thous.} = 10 \text{ ten thous.} = 1 \text{ h'd th.} = 100000.$$
$$10 \times 1 \text{ hund. th.} = 10 \text{ hund. thous.} = 1 \text{ million} = 1000000.$$

In the same way:

$$1 \times 2 \text{ units} = 2 \text{ units} = 2$$
$$10 \times 2 \text{ "} = 20 \text{ "} = 20$$
$$10 \times 2 \text{ tens} = 20 \text{ tens} = 200$$
$$\text{etc.}$$

$$1 \times 3 \text{ units} = 3 \text{ units} = 3$$
$$10 \times 3 \text{ "} = 30 \text{ "} = 30$$
$$10 \times 3 \text{ tens} = 30 \text{ "} = 300$$
$$\text{etc.}$$

1 unit   = 1 × 1 unit
1 ten   = 10 × 1 unit   = 10 units.
1 hundred = 10 × 1 ten   = 100 units.
1 thousand = 10 × 1 hundred = 100 × 1 ten = 1000 units.
                              etc.

The units are units of the first order, the tens are units of the second order, the hundreds are units of the third order, etc. The units of each order are 10 times more than the units of the preceding order. In each order there can be only 10 units, and the tenth unit is the first of the following order.

b. (Written.)

We will write the number 1852, placing the units, tens, hundreds, and thousands, each in a separate box.

Counting from the right towards the left, we have units in the first box, tens in the second, hundreds in the third and thousands in the fourth, tens of thousands in the fifth, hundreds of thousands in the sixth, millions in the seventh.

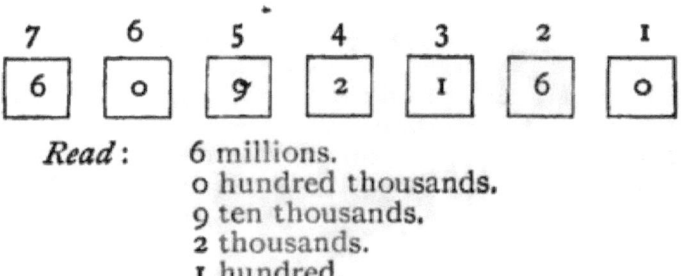

Read :   6 millions.
              0 hundred thousands.
              9 ten thousands.
              2 thousands.
              1 hundred.
              6 tens.
              0 units.

Or,

              6 million 92 thousand 1 hundred and 60.

Give the name of the units of the 1st, 3d, 5th, 4th, 6th order.

What are units of the 8th order called? etc., etc.

Then the teacher writes 9 in each box successively, and the children read it.

8	7	6	5	4	3	2	1
							9
						9	o
					9	o	o
				9	o	o	o
			9	o	o	o	o
		9	o	o	o	o	o
	9	o	o	o	o	o	o
9	o	o	o	o	o	o	o

Again the teacher writes and the children read :

90,000,000
9,000,000
900,000
90,000
9,000
900
90
9

Instead of boxes columns may be used as follows. The teacher writes, and the children read :

9 H. Mil.	8 T. Millions	7 Millions	6 H. Thous.	5 T. Thous.	4 Thous.	3 Hund.	2 Tens.	1 Units.
3	0	5	6	4	8	7	0	0
	2	6	5	9	0	8	4	
	7	0	0	9	3	6	4	2
				1	9	8	6	0

The pupils should arrange such columns on their slates, and on the blackboard then write numbers in them from dictation. They must also be drilled in such exercises as:

What is the 3d order, the 5th, the 8th, the 6th, the 4th, etc.?

The hundreds are what order? The millions? The tens of thousands?

The orders must be known from right to left and left to right, so as to be given without hesitation with great facility.

Then the numbers may be divided into periods (threes), attention being called to the fact that there are "units," "tens," and "hundreds" of units; also units, tens, and hundreds of thousands, millions, etc.

The periods may be shown as follows:

Million.			Thousand.			Units.		
h.	t.	u.	h.	t.	u.	h.	t.	u.
3	2	5	1	7	6	1	8	0

Then all columns, etc., may be abandoned, and the numbers written in periods. Always have the commas, which separate the periods, placed in at the time of writing the number, and not after all the figures have been written. Thus: 325 million (comma), 176 thousand (comma), 180. Thus the pupil becomes perfectly sure in both writing and reading numbers.

SECOND STEP.

Addition.

ORAL AND WRITTEN.

a. Numbers of one figure :

4 units + 5 units = 9 units (4 + 5 = 9).
4 tens + 5 tens = 9 tens = 90 (40 + 50 = 90).
4 hund. + 5 hund. = 9 hund. = 900 (400 + 500 = 900).
4 th. + 5 th = 9 th. = 9,000 (4,000 + 5,000 = 9,000).
4 ten th. + 5 ten th. = 9 ten th. = 90,000 (40,000 + 50,000 = 90,000).

etc.

b. Numbers of two figures and one figure :

43 units + 5 units = 48 units (43 + 5 = 48).
43 tens + 5 tens = 48 tens = 480 (430 + 50 = 480).
etc.

c. Numbers of two figures and two figures :

43 units + 28 units = 71 units (43 + 28 = 71).
43 tens + 28 tens = 71 tens = 710 (430 + 280 = 710).
etc.

d. Numbers of three figures and one figure :

416 units + 8 units = 424 units (416 + 8 = 424).
416 tens + 8 tens = 424 tens = 4,240 (4,160 + 80 = 4,240).
etc.

e. Numbers of three figures and two figures :

416 units + 23 units = 439 units (416 + 23 = 439).
416 tens + 23 tens = 439 tens = 4,390 (4,160 + 230 = 4,390).
416 hund. + 23 hund. = 439 hund. = 43,900 (41,600 + 2,300 = 43,900).
416 th. + 23 th. = 439 th. = 439,000 (416,000 + 23,000 = 439,000).
etc.

f. Numbers of three figures and three figures :

416 units + 123 units = 539 units (416 + 123 × 539).
416 tens + 123 tens = 539 tens = 5,390 (4,160 + 1,230
= 5,390).
416 hund. + 123 hund. = 539 hund. = 53,900 (41,600 +
12,300 = 53,900).

etc.

The corresponding method for operations to acquire
rapidity.   For examples :

a. 7   + 8   + 9   + 6
  70   + 80   + 90   + 60
  700   + 800   + 900   + 600
  7000   + 8000   + 9000   + 6000
  70000   + 80000   + 90000   + 60000
etc.

b.   25   + 9   + 3   + 8
  250   + 90   + 30   + 80
  2500 + 900 + 300 + 800
etc.

c.   25   + 36   + 47   + 58
  250   + 360   + 470   + 580
  2500 + 3600 + 4700 + 5800
etc.

d.   254   + 6   + 8   + 9
  2540   + 60   + 80   + 90
  25400 + 600 + 800 + 900
etc.

e.   254   + 27   + 38   + 49
  2540   + 270   + 380   + 490
  25400 + 2700 + 3800 + 4900
etc.

f.   254   + 316   + 449
  2540   + 3160   + 4490
  25400 + 31600 + 44900
etc.

The pupils must be led step by step in written addition as well as oral.

Let them write in columns:

(1)

	36	Shorter:	36
	24		24
	15		15
	23		23
	50		50
	18 units		148
	13 tens		
	148 units		

(2)

	365	or	365	Shorter:	365
	21		21		21
	1430		1430		1430
	2045		2045		2045
	320		320		320
	3000		11		4181
	1000		170		
	170		1000		
	11		3000		
	4181		4181		

(3)

	5946	5946	5 9 4 6
	847	847	8 4 7
	239	239	2 3 9
	6320	6320	6 3 2 0
			(2)(1)(2)
	11000	22	1 3 3 5 2
	2200	130	
	130	2200	
	22	11000	
	13352	13352	

(Place the number to be "carried" under the column to which it belongs, in parenthesis, using smaller figure.)

Pupils should be able to answer promptly questions on the addition processes.

THIRD STEP.

Subtraction.

ORAL AND WRITTEN.

a. Numbers of one figure:

9 units — 5 units = 4 units (9 — 5 = 4).
9 tens — 5 tens = 4 tens (90 — 50 = 40).
9 hund. — 5 hund. = 4 hund. (900 — 500 = 400).
etc.

b. Numbers of two figures with one figure:

12 units — 5 units = 7 units (12 — 5 = 7).
12 tens — 5 tens = 7 tens (120 = 50 = 70).
12 hund. — 5 hund. = 7 hund. (1200 — 500 = 700).
etc.

Continue in the same manner as in addition.
From 9456 take 7321.

$$a. \quad \begin{aligned} 9456 &= 9000 + 400 + 50 + 6 = 9456 \\ 7321 &= 7000 + 300 + 20 + 1 = 7321 \\ \hline & 2000 + 100 + 30 + 5 = 2135 \end{aligned}$$

b.   4325 — 1123 = 4325 Minuend.
                1123 Subtrahend.
                ———
                3202 Remainder.

c. (Borrowing without ciphers.)

(1)
$$\begin{array}{r} {}^{16}\ {}^{15}\ {}^{18} \\ 1\ \ 7 \cdot 6 \cdot 8* \\ 6\ \ 7\ \ 9 \\ \hline 1\ 0\ 8\ 9 \end{array} \quad = \quad \begin{array}{r} 1768 \\ 679 \\ \hline 1089 \end{array}$$

(2)
$$\begin{array}{r} {}^{13}\ {}^{12} \\ 4\ 5 \cdot 4 \cdot 2 \\ 4\ 1\ 5\ 9 \\ \hline 3\ 8\ 3 \end{array} \quad = \quad \begin{array}{r} 4\ 5\ 4\ 2 \\ 4\ 1\ 5\ 9 \\ \hline 3\ 8\ 3 \end{array}$$

---

* Grubé placed dots at the bottom where "borrowing" was employed; but in order to avoid confusing them with the later use of the decimal point, we place them at the top. The Germans use the comma for the decimal point, therefore this danger does not arise with them.

Where "borrowing" is necessary, make the necessary changes in the minuend, placing smaller figures above to indicate the changes. Then work the same example without making the changes.

d. (Borrowing with ciphers.)

(1)
$$
\begin{array}{r}
\overset{\scriptstyle 15\ 10}{7\ 4\cdot 6\cdot 0} \\
3\ 2\ 6\ 9 \\
\hline
4\ 1\ 9\ 1
\end{array}
=
\begin{array}{r}
7\ 4\ 6\ 0 \\
3\ 2\ 6\ 9 \\
\hline
4\ 1\ 9\ 1
\end{array}
$$

(9 units cannot be taken from o units, so I borrow from the tens; that is, take one from the 6 tens, which I indicate by a point after the 6. The ten taken away = 10 units. 9 units from 10 units = 1 unit; etc.)

(2)
$$
\begin{array}{r}
\overset{\scriptstyle 9}{\underset{}{}} \\[-1ex]
\overset{\scriptstyle 10\ 16}{7\ 4\cdot 0\cdot 6} \\
3\ 2\ 6\ 9 \\
\hline
4\ 1\ 3\ 7
\end{array}
=
\begin{array}{r}
7\ 4\cdot 0\ 6 \\
3\ 2\ 6\ 9 \\
\hline
4\ 1\ 3\ 7
\end{array}
$$

(3)
$$
\begin{array}{r}
\overset{\scriptstyle 9}{\underset{}{}} \\[-1ex]
\overset{\scriptstyle 10\ 13\ 16}{7\cdot 0\ 4\cdot 6} \\
3\ 2\ 6\ 9 \\
\hline
3\ 7\ 7\ 7
\end{array}
=
\begin{array}{r}
7\cdot 0\ 4\cdot 6 \\
3\ 2\ 6\ 9 \\
\hline
3\ 7\ 7\ 7
\end{array}
$$

(4)
$$
\begin{array}{r}
\overset{\scriptstyle 9}{\underset{}{}} \\[-1ex]
\overset{\scriptstyle 10\ 10}{7\ 4\cdot 0\ 0} \\
3\ 2\ 6\ 9 \\
\hline
4\ 1\ 3\ 1
\end{array}
=
\begin{array}{r}
7\ 4\cdot 0\ 0 \\
3\ 2\ 6\ 9 \\
\hline
4\ 1\ 3\ 1
\end{array}
$$

(5)
$$
\begin{array}{r}
\overset{\scriptstyle 9\ 9}{\underset{}{}} \\[-1ex]
\overset{\scriptstyle 6\ 10\ 10\ 14}{7\cdot 0\ 0\ 4} \\
3\ 2\ 6\ 9 \\
\hline
3\ 7\ 3\ 5
\end{array}
=
\begin{array}{r}
7\cdot 0\ 0\ 4 \\
3\ 2\ 6\ 9 \\
\hline
3\ 7\ 3\ 5
\end{array}
$$

$$\begin{array}{c} \overset{9\ 9}{\underset{10\ 10\ 10}{}} \\ 7\text{·}0\ 0\ 0 \\ 3\ 2\ 6\ 9 \end{array} = \begin{array}{c} 7\text{·}0\ 0\ 0 \\ 3\ 2\ 6\ 9 \end{array}$$

(6)

$$3\ 7\ 3\ 1 \qquad 3\ 7\ 3\ 1$$

(7)

$$\begin{array}{c} \overset{9\ 9\ 9}{\underset{10\ 10\ 10\ 16}{}} \\ 7\text{·}0\ 0\ 0\ 6 \\ 3\ 2\ 6\ 9\ 7 \end{array} = \begin{array}{c} 7\text{·}0\ 0\ 0\ 6 \\ 3\ 2\ 6\ 9\ 7 \end{array}$$

$$3\ 7\ 3\ 0\ 9 \qquad 3\ 7\ 3\ 0\ 9$$

This kind of work must not be left until the pupil is able to perform it rapidly. He must understand that as 7 units cannot be taken from 6 units, he must borrow of the tens. As there are no tens, hundreds, or thousands, he must go to the tens of thousands to borrow, and reducing one of this to the next lower denomination, then borrowing from that, etc., until we come to the order where we need to increase the minuend figure.

The explanation of subtraction is based on addition. Take two numbers :

$$\begin{array}{ll} a. & 3480 \\ b. & 2375 \quad \text{Adding.} \\ \hline c. & 5855 \end{array}$$

How large is *a*?   ($a = 5855 - 2375.$)
How large is *b*?   ($b = 5855 - 3480.$)
How was *c* found?   (By adding *a* and *b*.)

How were *a* or *b* found?   (By subtracting the known *a* or *b* from their sum *c*.)

What do we call *c* in this subtraction?   (The minuend.)
What do we call the *a* or *b*?   (The subtrahend.)
What do we seek?   (The remainder or difference.)

If the minuend were unknown how would you find it? (By adding the subtrahend and difference.)

$$\begin{array}{r} 5855 \\ -\ 3480 \\ \hline 2375 \\ +\ 3480 \\ \hline 5855 \end{array} \qquad \begin{array}{r} 5855 \\ -\ 2375 \\ \hline 3480 \\ +\ 2375 \\ \hline 5855 \end{array} \Big\} \text{ Proof.}$$

How can I prove subtraction?

What is the whole in an example in subtraction called? (The minuend.)

In addition? (The sum.)

What is the difference between addition and subtraction? (In addition the parts are given from which the whole is to be found; in subtraction the whole and one of the parts are given from which the other part is to be found.)

The sum 5855 is composed of three numbers; the first = 1320, the second = 1427; what is the third?

$$5855 - 1320 - 1427 = 5855 - (1320 + 1427.)$$

		Proof:
5855	1320	3108
1320	+ 1427	+ $\begin{cases} 1320 \\ 1427 \end{cases}$
———	———	———
4535	2747	5855
1427		
———	5855	
3108	− 2747	
	———	
	3108	

FOURTH STEP.

Multiplication.

ORAL AND WRITTEN.

1. Multiplier One Figure.

a. Multiplicand One Figure.

3 × 9 units = 27 units (3 × 9 = 27).
3 × 9 tens = 27 tens (3 × 90 = 270).
3 × 9 hund. = 27 hund. (3 × 900 = 2700).
etc.

b. Multiplicand Two Figures.

3 × 29 units = 87 units (3 × 29 = 3 × 20 = 60
3 × 9 = 27
———
87).

3 × 29 tens = 87 tens (3 × 290 = 870).
3 × 29 hund. = 87 hund. (3 × 2900 = 8700).

c. Multiplicand Three Figures.

3 × 529 units = 1587 units (3 × 500 = 1500
            3 × 20 = 60
            3 × 9 = 27
            ————
            1587).

3 × 529 tens = 1587 tens (3 × 5290 = 15870).
            etc.

d. Multiplicand Four Figures.

3 × 5293 units = 15879 units (3 × 5000 = 15000
            3 × 200 = 600
            3 × 90 = 270
            3 × 3 = 9
            ————
            15879).

3 × 5293 tens = 15879 tens (3 × 52930 = 158790).
3 × 5293 hund. = 15879 hund. (3 × 529300 = 1587900).

2. Multiplier Two Figures.

a. THE PURE TENS.

1. *Multiplicand One Figure.*

60 × 5 units = 300 units (60 × 5 = 300).
60 × 5 tens = 300 tens (60 × 50 = 3000).
60 × 5 hund. = 300 hund. (60 × 500 = 30000).
60 × 5 thous. = 300 thous. (60 × 5000 = 300000).

2. *Multiplicand Two Figures.*

60 × 56 units = 3360 units (60 × 50 = 3000
            60 × 6 = 360
            ————
            3360).

60 × 56 tens = 3360 tens (60 × 560 = 33600).
            etc.

3. *Multiplicand Three Figures.*

60 × 562 units = 33720 units (60 × 500 = 30000
                              60 × 60 = 3600
                              60 × 2 = 120
                              ————————
                              33720).

60 × 562 tens = 33720 tens (60 × 5620 = 337200).

b. MIXED TENS.

(1) 25 × 9 units = 225 units (20 × 9 = 180
                             5 × 9 = 45
                             ————
                             225).   ∎

25 × 9 tens = 225 tens (25 × 90 = 2250).

(2) 25 × 96 units = 2400 units (20 × 96 = 1920
                               5 × 96 = 480
                               ————
                               2400).

25 × 96 tens = 2400 tens (25 × 960 = 24000).

3. Multiplier Three Figures.

a. PURE HUNDREDS.

1. *Multiplicand One Figure.*

300 × 9 units = 2700 units (300 × 9 = 2700).
300 × 9 tens = 2700 tens (300 × 90 = 27000).
300 × 9 hund. = 2700 hund. (300 × 900 = 270000).

2. *Multiplicand Two Figures.*

300 × 91 units = 27300 units (300 × 90 = 27000
                             300 × 1 = 300
                             ————————
                             27300

300 × 91 tens = 27300 tens (300 × 910 = 273000).

3. *Multiplicand Three Figures.*

300 × 914 units = 274200 units (300 × 900 = 270000

$$300 \times 10 = 3000$$
$$300 \times 4 = 1200$$

$$\overline{274200}).$$

300 × 914 tens = 274200 tens (300 × 9140 = 2742000).

b. MIXED HUNDREDS.

304 × 9 units = 2736 units (300 × 9 = 2700

$$4 \times 9 = 36$$

$$\overline{2736})$$

304 × 9 tens = 2736 tens (304 × 90 = 27360).
304 × 9 hund. = 2736 hund. (304 × 900 = 273600).

This will be sufficient to illustrate the method. Practice must be given in rapid reckoning—
a. In connection with addition and subtraction.
b. In multiplication alone.

Method for Slate Work.

1. *Multiplier One Figure.*

(1) No carrying:

$$3 \times 3213 = 3 \times 3000 = 9000$$
$$3 \times 200 = 600$$
$$3 \times 10 = 30$$
$$3 \times 3 = 9$$

$$\overline{9639}$$

Shorter: Shortest:
3213   3213
   3   3
————   ————
   9   9639
  30
 600
9000
————
9639

(2) Carrying:

$$3 \times 3226 = 3 \times 3000 = 9000$$
$$3 \times 200 = 600$$
$$3 \times 20 = 60$$
$$3 \times 6 = 18$$

$$9678$$

3226	3226
3	3
18	9678
60	
600	
9000	
9678	

(3) Cipher in Multiplication:

$$3 \times 4046 = 3 \times 4000 = 12000$$
$$3 \times 40 = 120$$
$$3 \times 6 = 18$$

$$12138$$

4046	4046
3	3
18	12138
120	
12000	
12138	

$$3 \times 32130 = (3 \times 3213) \times 10$$

3213
3

9639 $10 \times 9639 = 96390$

Therefore: $3 \times 32130 = 96390$.

The pupil will learn that every time a cipher is added to the product, it is multiplied by 10. Therefore it follows that when the multiplier is tens, hundreds, etc., they may be treated as units and as many ciphers added to the result as the order requires.

For example :

$$345 \times 2068 = 2068$$
$$345$$
$$\overline{}$$
$$10340$$
$$8272(0)$$
$$6204(00)$$
$$\overline{}$$
$$713460$$

Explanation of Multiplication.

How many times must I take 112 to get 336?

$$112$$
$$112$$
$$112$$
$$\overline{}$$
$$336$$

How can I express that shorter?

$$3 \times 112 = 336.$$

$$112 \; a.$$
$$3 \; b.$$
$$\overline{}$$
$$336 \; c.$$

How many numbers have I?
Which number is the entirety? (*c*.)
What is the *a*? (A part of *c*.)
What does the *b* tell us? (How many times we must take the part *a* in order to get *c*.)
What is *c*? (The product.)
How do we get *c* from *a*?

What do we call the number which we multiply in order to get the product?

What is the multiplicand? Multiplier? Product?

The multiplicand and multiplier are **together** called factors, because they produce the product.

What are the factors of 620, 1000?

If $336 = 3 \times 112$, how many times must I be able to subtract 112 from 336?

$$
\begin{array}{r}
33\dot{6} \\
-\ 112 \\
\hline
224 \\
-\ 112 \\
\hline
112 \\
-\ 112 \\
\hline
000
\end{array}
$$

The pupil must be able to **explain** multiplication somewhat as follows:

$$209 \times 3148 = ?$$

The multiplicand is 3148. This is a part of the unknown product. The multiplier is 209, and tells me how many times I must take the multiplicand 3148 in order to get the product. I take therefore 3148 209 times. I multiply first by 9 units and get 28,332. I proceed to the tens, and as there are none, pass on to the hundreds. I multiply 3148 by 2, and this product by 100, and this gives me 629600. Add the products, and I get 657,932, the product of 209×3148.

$$
\begin{array}{r}
3148 \\
209 \\
\hline
28332 \\
6296 \\
\hline
657932
\end{array}
$$

It should by shown that the factors may change places without changing the result.

312 (*a*)	113 (*a*)
113 (*b*)	312 (*b*)
———	———
936	226
312	113
312	339
———	———
35256 (*c*)	35256 (*c*)

FIFTH STEP.

Division.

ORAL AND WRITTEN.

A.—Without Remainder.

I. DIVISOR ONE FIGURE.

(Quotient unchanged.)

a. Dividend also One Figure.

3 units in 6 units $= 2$ $(6 \div 3 = 2)$.
3 tens in 6 tens $= 2$ $(60 \div 30 = 2)$.
3 hund. in 6 hund. $= 2$ $(600 \div 300 = 2)$.
etc.

b. Dividend Two Figures.

3 units in 18 units $= 6$ $(18 \div 3 = 6)$.
3 tens in 18 tens $= 6$ $(180 \div 30 = 6)$.
3 hund. in 18 hund. $= 6$ $(1800 \div 300 = 6)$.
etc.

c. Dividend Three Figures.

3 units in 186 units $= 62$ $(186 \div 3 = 62)$.
3 tens in 186 tens $= 62$ $(1860 \div 30 = 62)$.
3 hund. in 186 hund. $= 62$ $(18600 \div 300 = 62)$.
etc.

(Quotient increasing according to decimal scale.)

a. One third of 6 units $= 2$ units $(6 \div 3 = 2)$.
One third of 6 tens $= 2$ tens $(60 \div 3 = 20)$.
One third of 6 hund. $= 2$ hund. $(600 \div 3 = 200)$.

b. One third of 18 units = 6 units (18 ÷ 3 = 6).
One third of 18 tens = 6 tens (180 ÷ 3 = 60).

c. One third of 186 units = 62 units (186 ÷ 3 = 62).
One third of 186 tens = 62 tens (1860 ÷ 3 = 620).

2. DIVISOR TWO FIGURES.

(Quotient the same.)

a. Dividend also Two Figures.

18 units in 54 units = 3 (54 ÷ 18 = 3).
18 tens in 54 tens = 3 (540 ÷ 180 = 3).
18 hund. in 54 hund. = 3 (5400 ÷ 1800 = 3).

b. Dividend Three Figures.

18 units in 108 units = 6 (108 ÷ 18 = 6).
18 tens in 108 tens = 6 (1080 ÷ 180 = 6).

(Quotient increasing.)

a. $\frac{1}{18}$ of 54 units = 3 units (54 ÷ 18 = 3).
$\frac{1}{18}$ of 54 tens = 3 tens (540 ÷ 18 = 30).
$\frac{1}{18}$ of 54 hund. = 3 hund. (5400 ÷ 18 = 300).

b. $\frac{1}{18}$ of 108 units = 6 units (108 ÷ 18 = 6).
$\frac{1}{18}$ of 108 tens = 6 tens (1080 ÷ 18 = 60).
etc.

3. DIVISOR THREE FIGURES.

(Quotient the same.)

a. Dividend also Three Figures.

114 units in 342 units = 3 (342 ÷ 114 = 3).
114 tens in 342 tens = 3 (3420 ÷ 1140 = 3).
etc.

b. Dividend Four Figures.

506 units in 1012 units = 2 (1012 ÷ 506 = 2).
506 tens in 1012 tens = 2 (10120 ÷ 5060 = 2).

(Quotient increasing.)

a. $\frac{1}{114}$ of 342 units = 3 units (342 ÷ 114 = 3).
$\frac{1}{114}$ of 342   tens = 3 tens   (3420 ÷ 114 = 30).
etc.

b. $\frac{1}{506}$ of 1012 units = 2 units (1012 ÷ 506 = 2).
$\frac{1}{506}$ of 1012 tens   = 2 tens   (10120 ÷ 506 = 20).
etc.

B.—With Remainder.

I. DIVISOR ONE FIGURE.

(Quotient also one figure.)

a. *Dividend One Figure.*

3 units in 7 units = 2 with 1 unit remainder (7 ÷ 3 = 2 [1]).

3 tens in 7 tens = 2 with 1 ten remainder (70 ÷ 30 = 2 [10]).

3 hund. in 7 hund. = 2 with 1 hund. remainder (700 ÷ 300 = 2 [100]).

b. *Dividend Two Figures.*

3 units in 25 units = 8 with 1 unit remainder (25 ÷ 3 = 8 [1]).

3 tens in 25 tens = 8 with 1 ten remainder (250 ÷ 30 = 8 [10]).

etc.

The teacher will easily continue this work according to the plan followed in the preceding pages under **A.**

Rapid reckoning must not be neglected.

$\frac{1}{16}$ of 48 is what part of 120?

$\frac{1}{509}$ × 1018 divided by 2 is what part of 100?

$\frac{1}{4}$ × 9600 ÷ 2 is contained how many times in 9600?

8000 ÷ 800 × 3 × ($\frac{1}{3}$ × 16) is how many times 12?

3 × 120 ÷ 6 × 5 ÷ 15 × 4 ÷ 16?

55 ÷ 18, the remainder 9 times is contained how many times in 5409?

etc.

METHOD FOR WRITTEN DIVISION.

A.—Without Remainder.

I. DIVISOR ONE FIGURE.

a. *Dividend Without Ciphers.*

$$15936 \div 3 = 3 \text{ into } 15000 + 900 + 30 + 6.$$

```
3 into 15000 =  5000        Shorter:
3  "     900 =   300     3 into 15936 = 5000
3  "      30 =    10         15000       300
3  "       6 =     2         ------        10
   -------------------         936         2
3  "   15936 =  5312          900        ----
                              ----       5312
                               36
                               30
                               --
                                6
                                6
                                -
```

```
       Shorter:
3 into 15936 = 5...      or,    3 into 15936(5312
       15...      3..                 15...
       ------      1.                 ------
         9..       2                    9..
         9..      ----                   9..
         ---      5312                  ---
          3.                             3.
          3.                             3.
          --                             --
           6                              6
                                          6
                                          -
```

The shortest :   3)15936 the whole.

                  5312 the part.

Or in fractional form : $\dfrac{15936}{3} = 5312.$

```
6 into 49686(8 ...         or,      6 into 49686(8281
       48000  2 ..                         48 ...
       ─────   8 .                         ─────
       1686   1                            16 ..
       1200  ─────                         12 ..
       ─────  8281                         ─────
        486                                 48 .
        480                                 48 .
       ─────                               ─────
          6                                   6
          6                                   6
       ─────                               ─────
          ─
```

In fractional form : $\dfrac{49686}{6} = 8281$

b. Dividend with Ciphers.

```
8 into 650048(80000
       640000  1000
       ──────   200
       10048    50
        8000    6
       ──────  ─────
        2048  81256
        1600
       ──────
         448
         400
       ──────
          48
          48
       ──────
          ──
```

($\frac{1}{8}$ of 65 ten thous. = 8 ten thous.   8 × 8 ten thous. = 64 ten thous.   64 ten thous. from 65 ten thous. leaves 1 ten thous. $\frac{1}{8}$ of 10 thous. = 1 thous., etc.)

```
8)650048(81256        8)664800(83100
  64 .... ·····          64 .... ·····
  ─────                  ─────
  10 ...                 24 ...
   8 ...                 24 ...
  ─────                  ─────
  20 ..                   8 ..
  16 ..                   8 ..
  ─────                  ─────
  44 .                    00
  40 .
  ─────
     48
     48
     ──
```

c. Divisor with Ciphers.

10 into 664800 = 10 into 600,000 + 60,000 + 4000 + 800.

```
10 into 60000|0 = 60000
10   "   6000|0 =  6000
10   "    400|0 =   400
10   "     80|0 =    80
────────────────────────
10 into 66480|0 = 66480
```

Every time a cipher is cut off, the number is divided by 10, for it makes the number just so many orders lower.

```
8ȼ)6648ȼȼ(8310
   64 ...
   ─────
   24 ..
   24 ..
   ─────
    8 .
    8 .
    ──
     0
     0
     ─
```

100)664800 = 6648

$$8\cancel{0}\cancel{0})6648\cancel{0}\cancel{0}(831$$
$$64..$$
$$\overline{}$$
$$24.$$
$$24.$$
$$\overline{}$$
$$8$$
$$8$$
$$\overline{-}$$

$$= \frac{6648\cancel{0}\cancel{0}}{8\cancel{0}\cancel{0}} = 831$$

B.—With Remainder.

(Same plan as with **A**.)

a.   59634 + 7.

59634 = 59000 + 600 + 30 + 4.

7 into 59000 = 8000
     56000
     ―――――
     3000
   + 600
     ―――――
   7)3600 = .500
     3500
     ―――――
     100
   + 30
     ―――――
   7)130 =   10
      70
     ―――――
      60
    + 4
     ―――――
   7)64 =   9
     63
     ―――――
   7) 1 = $\frac{1}{7}$

$= 8519\frac{1}{7}$

```
7)59634(8519 1/7
  56...  ....
  ----
   36..
   35..
   ---
    13.
     7.
    --
     64
     63
     --
     1/7
```

or $\frac{59634}{7} = 8519\frac{1}{7}$

b. 9 into 735040(81671 1/9

```
 72....
 ------
  15...
   9...
  -----
   60..
   54..
   ----
    64.
    63.
    ---
     10
      9
     --
     1/9
```

$\frac{735040}{9} = 81671\frac{1}{9}$

c. 90 into 735040(8167 1/9

```
 72...
 -----
  15..
   9..
  ----
   60.
   54.
   ---
    64
    63
    --
    1/9
```

$\frac{735040}{90} = \frac{73504}{9} = 8167\frac{1}{9}$

$9\not{0})73504\not{0} = \frac{73504}{9} = 8167\frac{1}{9}$

$$90)73504(816\tfrac{6\,4}{9\,0}$$
$$72000 \cdots$$

$$\begin{array}{r} 1504 \\ 900 \\ \hline 604 \\ 540 \\ \hline \tfrac{6\,4}{9\,0} \end{array}$$

$$900)735040 = \dfrac{73504}{90} = 816\tfrac{6\,4}{9\,0}$$

In the same manner the teacher will be able to continue these operations, completing all the steps in division. Care must be taken that the pupil be always clear and prompt, when called upon to explain his operations.

EXPLANATION OF DIVISION.

The teacher in explaining division must start with multiplication.

$$\begin{array}{rl} 1260 & (a) \\ 3 & \times\ (b) \\ \hline 3780 & (c) \end{array}$$

What is c? (The product or whole.)
What is a? (The multiplicand, a part of the whole.)
What is b? (The multiplier, which tells me how many times the multiplicand is to be taken.)
Find a from b and c.

$$\begin{array}{c} (b)\ (c)\ \ (a) \\ 3)3780(1260 \\ 3\cdots \\ \hline 7\,\cdot\cdot \\ 6\,\cdot\cdot \\ \hline 18\,. \\ 18\,. \\ \hline 0 \end{array}$$

The product or entirety is the dividend; the number that I divide by is the divisor, and the number sought, or result, is the quotient.

$$c = \text{dividend,}$$
$$b = \text{divisor,}$$
$$a = \text{quotient.}$$

What are a and b with reference to the product or dividend? (Factors.)
What are given in division?
(The product and one factor.)
What must be found? (The other factor.)
How is that done? (By division.)
If a were the known factor, how shall b be found?

$$1260)3780(3$$
$$3780$$
$$\overline{}$$

How many times can I take 1260 from 3780?

$$3780$$
$$-\ 1260$$
$$\overline{}$$
$$2520$$
$$-\ 1260$$
$$\overline{}$$
$$1260$$
$$-\ 1260$$
$$\overline{}$$

What number is found 3 times in 3780?
The pupil must be able to give an explanation similar to the following:
The number which is contained 3 times in 3780 must be $\frac{1}{3}$ of 3780. I find $\frac{1}{3}$ of 3780 by dividing it by 3. The divisor 3 is the known factor; the dividend 3780, the product and the quotient is the unknown factor, which will be found when I divide the product by the known factor.
$3780 = 37$ hund. and 8 tens; $\frac{1}{3}$ of 37 hund. $= 12$ hund. with remainder of 1 hund.; 1 hund. $+$ 8 tens $= 18$ tens; $\frac{1}{3}$ of 18 tens $= 6$ tens.
Therefore $\frac{1}{3}$ of 3780 $= 12$ hund. $+$ 6 tens $= 1260$. The quotient 1260 is the number which is contained 3 times in 3780. Therefore 1260 can be taken 3 times from 3780.

CONCRETE NUMBERS.

We now need no especial explanation of the application to concrete numbers either for the teacher or for the pupils. It is recommended that there shall always be oral exercises first, before the blackboard or slate be used, until the pupils are familiar with the expressions.

1. ADDITION.

How many times does the clock strike in 24 hours?

a. What is given in this example?

(24 hours, the time in which the clock strikes.)

What do you know about the striking of the clock?

(The clock strikes 1 at one o'clock, 2 at two o'clock, 3 at three o'clock, etc., till 12, and then it begins to strike 1, 2, 3, etc., again to 12.)

b. What is required?

(The number of strokes of the clock in 24 hours.)

As the clock strikes only 12, how shall the reckoning be done?

(Find the number of strokes for 12 hours.)

Then how do you find the number for 24 hours?

(By taking the number for 12 hours twice.)

c. How many strokes for 12 hours?

$(1 + 2 + 3 + 4 + 5 + 6 + 7 + 8 + 9 + 10 + 11 + 12 = 78$ strokes.)

How many for 24 hours? $(2 \times 78 = 156$ strokes.)

How does the number of strokes for 24 hours compare with those for 12 hours?

How does the number of strokes for the first 11 hours compare with those of the 12 hours? Of the 12th hour?

How many strokes have there been at the 15th hour?

$(78 + 1 + 2 + 3 = 84$ strokes.)

Give a variety of concrete examples.

2. SUBTRACTION.

The property of a man before a fire consisted of 34580 dollars. After it he had only 6594 dollars.

How much did he lose?

a. How do you see already that the man has lost by the fire?

(He had more money before the fire than after it.)

How much must he have had after the fire in order to be able to say that he had lost nothing?

(He must have had 34580 dollars.)

But how much had he?   (He had only 6594 dollars.)

b. What would you call his loss if he counted his money and found only $6594? *

(What this lacks of $34580.)

Concerning what is the question?   (The loss.)

How much must the man add to $6594 in order to get $34580?

c. How do you find that?

(By adding to $6594, until I get $34580; or by subtracting 6594 from 34580.)

Do the first.

6594 = 65 hund. + 94 units; I make the 66 hundreds complete by adding 6 units. As 34580 = 345 hund. + 80 units, I must have with the 66 hund. 34 hund. + 245 hund. + 80 units more.   34 hund. + 245 hund. = 279 hund.; to the 80 units must be added also 6 units = 86 units.   So I must add to 6594 279 hund. + 86 units = 27986 in order to get 34580.   Therefore the man must have lost 27986 dollars.

How can you express the loss by using the numbers given in the example?

(The man had lost 34580 − 6594 dollars.)

The loss equalled what difference?

(The difference between his first and last amount of property.)

Show in the same way how much greater his loss was than what he still retained.

Suppose the loss to be known, and the later property unknown; what would the example then be?

(The property of a man was $34580. By a fire he lost $27986. How much had he still?)

In the same way suppose the property at first to be unknown. How would the example read?

---

* The use of the dollar sign can be taught here, if not earlier. Make the sign ($), and tell the children that it stands for dollars.

3. MULTIPLICATION.

A merchant bought 3900 cwt. of wares @ $36, and sold them again @ $42 per cwt. How much did he make out of the transaction?

a. What did the merchant do?
(He bought 3900 cwt. @ $36.)
What else did he do? (He sold 1 cwt. @ $42.)
What is the cost price and the selling price of 1 cwt.?
b. What do you find when the price of both are compared?
As the selling price is the greater, what do we find?
(A gain.)
How much is gained on 1 cwt.? (6 dollars.)
How do you find that?
What is required in the example?
(The gain of the whole transaction.)
That is how many cwt.? (3900.)
What do you know of the gain?
(That 6 dollars have been gained on 1 cwt.)
How do you find the entire gain? (3900 × 6 dollars.)
3900 × 6 = 6 × 3900 = 6 × 39 hund. = 6 × 30 hund. + 6 × 9 hund. = 180 hund. + 54 hund. = 234 hund. = 23400. Therefore $23400 is the entire gain.

1. What was the entire cost? Selling price? Gain?
2. The gain on 1 cwt. was $6. What was the selling price, the cost being $36? The selling price was $42, the gain $6. What was the cost? The entire gain was $23400, and the gain on 1 cwt. was $6. How many cwt. were there?
3. If the merchant had gained only $11700, what would have been the selling price per cwt.?
(If he gains $11700 on 3900 cwt., on 1 cwt. he gains $\frac{1}{3900}$ of $11700 = $3. Since 1 cwt. cost $36 and gain $3, he must have sold for $36 + $3 = $39 per cwt.)

4. DIVISION.

A gardener worked a week in a garden and received for his work 9 dollars and 60 cents. How much did he receive daily?

a. There are 6 working days, for which he receives 9 dollars and 60 cents.

b. We must find the reward of one day's labor.

c. If in 6 days he earned 9 dollars and 60 cents, in 1 day he will earn $\frac{1}{6}$ of that. $\frac{1}{6}$ of 9 dollars is 1 dollar, and 3 dollars remainder. 3 dollars = 30 dimes; $\frac{1}{6}$ of 30 dimes = 5 dimes; $\frac{1}{6}$ of 60 cents = 10 cents. Therefore he receives 1 dollar + 5 dimes, or 50 cents, + 10 cents = 1 dollar 60 cents per day.

If a workman receives \$1.60 for a day, how much does he receive per week?

A man earns \$9.60, earning \$1.60 per day. How long does he work?

How does the pay for a week compare with that of a day?

5. MIXED EXERCISES.

1. **Two merchants** compare their gain after a transaction. B said to A, "The half of your gain is one third of mine." A had gained \$605. How much had B gained?

a. What do you know of A's gain? (It is \$605.)

What do you know of B's gain?

(That $\frac{1}{3}$ of it = $\frac{1}{2}$ of A's.)

b. If you knew $\frac{1}{3}$ of B's gain, what could you easily find? (His whole gain.)

How much would it be? (3 × the one third.)

But we have been told of what amount, which is equal to $\frac{1}{3}$ of B's? ($\frac{1}{2}$ of A's gain.)

How much is that? ($\frac{605}{2}$ dollars = \$302.50.)

c. How much is B's gain? (3 × \$302.50 = \$907.50.)

a. B gained \$907.50; A. said, "$\frac{1}{3}$ of your gain = $\frac{1}{2}$ of mine." What was A's gain?

b. Two merchants compared gains and found that B's gain was $\frac{1}{2}$ greater than A's. A had gained \$605. How much B?

c. Two merchants compared gains, and A found that his gain was $\frac{1}{3}$ less than B's, whose gain was \$907.50.

d. Two merchants in comparing gains found that what A had gained twice B had gained 3 times. B had made \$907.50.

e. They also found that $\frac{2}{3}$ of B's gain = the whole of A's. B had made \$907.50. How much A?

2. Three persons divide 4 cwt. and 40 lbs., so that A receives 30 lbs. and B 20 lbs. more than C. How many pounds did C get?

(We subtract first what A and B receive extra, that is, 30 lbs. + 20 lbs. = 50 lbs. 440 lbs. — 50 lbs. = 390 lbs. ⅓ of 390 lbs. = 130 lbs., C's part. B receives 20 lbs. extra, making 150 lbs. A receives 30 lbs. extra, making 160 lbs.)

a. Three persons divided a quantity of corn so that A had 5 lbs. more than B, and B 10 lbs. more than C. B's part was 155 lbs. How much was A's? C's? What was the whole amount divided?

b. Three persons divided 440 lbs., so that A received 10 lbs. more than B, and C 20 lbs. less. What was the part of each?

c. 12 workmen work on a building, 4 carpenters and 8 masons. The carpenters receive each 40 cents a day more than the masons. The pay of all the workmen amounts to 25 dollars 60 cents a day. How much does each carpenter and each mason receive per day?

(4 × 40c. = $1.60. $25.60 — $1.60 = $24. $24 ÷ 12 = $2, what each mason receives. $2 + 40c. = $2.40, the pay of each carpenter.)

3. N bought cloth for a new coat, paying $3 a yard. The whole cost was $12; how many yards did he buy?

a. N bought cloth for a coat, paying $3 a yard. If he took 4 yards, what was the cost?

b. If he paid $12 for 4 yards, what was the cost per yard?

c. B took of the same kind of cloth 4¼ yards. How much must he pay?

(If he had taken 4 yards, the cost would be $12. ¼ yard costs ¼ × $3 = 75 cents. $12 + .75 = $12.75, the amount he must pay.)

The teacher should multiply examples embracing all of compound numbers, until the pupil is prompt and accurate in the work. Great attention must be paid to the solution of examples. One example solved understandingly is of more worth than a dozen solved mechanically, according to rule, without understanding the principles involved.

Third Course.

FRACTIONS.

THE FOURTH YEAR.

FIRST HALF OF THE YEAR.

GENERAL CONTEMPLATION OF THE FRACTION.

REMARKS.

1. As the pupil arrived at a perception of whole numbers by measuring them by the smallest unit, so will he come to comprehend fractions by constant reference to the number one from which they have arisen.

2. While heretofore the one has been considered as a part of other numbers, it will now be considered as a whole consisting of parts. These parts can be resolved into their elements. With reference to their whole they are called fractions.

3. As the pupil has learned from the first to consider whole numbers as fractions, in that he recognized them as parts of larger numbers, the following treatment of the real fraction (the broken unit) will offer no difficulty to him. The process is exactly the same as that he has used in whole numbers, namely, perception of the manifold relations in their organic unity.

4. As the different kinds of fractions depend upon their size, and their size upon the number of equal parts

into which the unit is divided, the different kinds of divisions may be considered as especial orders, namely, *descending lower orders*, as in whole numbers the *ascending higher orders* of the units, tens, hundreds, etc., are formed by taking unity ten times.

5. We treat in the first step the half, in the second step the third, etc., until the pupil through this natural development of his perception comes to the observation of the fraction.

6. We begin, as in the preceding courses, with general observation of the object, and practise in the same manner oral and written, pure and applied, blending addition, subtraction, etc., together, and treat the fraction analogous with the whole number under the following heads:

1. Contemplation of the pure number.

   a. Measuring.
   b. Comparing.
   c. Combining.

2. Application of the pure relation of number to all the fundamental rules.

First Step.

Halves.

1.

---

* (The line divided into parts is to be the standard illustration for fractions, though other things may also be used. Avoid withdrawing the attention by attractive objects, remembering that all of the attention given to the object is so much withdrawn from the subject in hand, namely, fractions. Give many practical examples, as the four processes are carried along together from the first.

In division of fractions, do not allow the pupil to speak of 2 divided by ½, 4 by ⅔, etc., as he cannot understand it at this period; but rather, how many times is ½ contained in 2, or ⅔ contained in 4? The child can be shown how many times ½ is contained in 2. It is better that the pupil read 4 ÷ ⅔: 4 is twice the third part of what number; or better, ⅔ are contained in 4 how many times?)

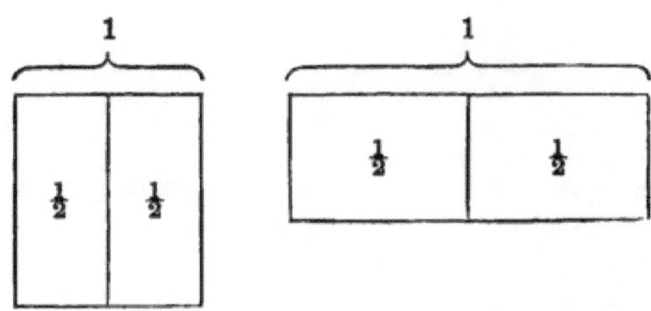

If I divide one (a whole) in two equal parts, I get 2 halves. One half is one of the 2 equal parts into which the whole is divided.

$$1 \div 2 = \tfrac{1}{2} \text{ or } \tfrac{1}{2} \times 1 = \tfrac{1}{2}.$$

MEASURING.

a. (Adding) $\tfrac{1}{2} + \tfrac{1}{2} = 1$.
b. (Multiplying) $1 \times \tfrac{1}{2} = \tfrac{1}{2}$, $2 \times \tfrac{1}{2} = 1$.
c. (Subtracting) $1 - \tfrac{1}{2} = \tfrac{1}{2}$.
d. (Dividing) $\tfrac{1}{2} + \tfrac{1}{2} = 1$, $1 \div \tfrac{1}{2} = 2$ ($\tfrac{1}{2}$ is contained in 1 twice).

APPLICATION.

a. Since $1 \div 2 = \tfrac{1}{2}$, $2 \div 2 = \tfrac{2}{2}$, $2 \div 3 = \tfrac{2}{3}$, $10 \div 2 = \tfrac{10}{2}$, $100 \div 2 = \tfrac{100}{2}$, etc.

ADDITION.

$\tfrac{1}{2} + \tfrac{1}{2} = 1$, $1 + \tfrac{1}{2} = 1\tfrac{1}{2}$, $2 + \tfrac{1}{2} = 2\tfrac{1}{2}$, $3 + \tfrac{1}{2} = 3\tfrac{1}{2}$, etc.; $1\tfrac{1}{2} + \tfrac{1}{2} = 2$, $2\tfrac{1}{2} + \tfrac{1}{2} = 3$, $12\tfrac{1}{2} + \tfrac{1}{2} = 13$, etc.; $1\tfrac{1}{2} + 1\tfrac{1}{2} = 3$ (for $1\tfrac{1}{2} + \tfrac{1}{2} = 2$, $+ 1 = 3$, or $1 + 1 = 2$, $\tfrac{1}{2} + \tfrac{1}{2} = 1$, $2 + 1 = 3$), $5\tfrac{1}{2} + 1\tfrac{1}{2} = 7$, $7\tfrac{1}{2} + 8 = 15\tfrac{1}{2}$, $7\tfrac{1}{2} + 8\tfrac{1}{2} = 16$, $8 + 8\tfrac{1}{2} = 16\tfrac{1}{2}$, etc.

MULTIPLICATION.

$2 \times \tfrac{1}{2} = \tfrac{2}{2} = 1$, $3 \times \tfrac{1}{2} = \tfrac{3}{2} = 1\tfrac{1}{2}$, $10 \times \tfrac{1}{2} = \tfrac{10}{2} = 5$, $100 \times \tfrac{1}{2} = \tfrac{100}{2} = 50$; $7 \times \tfrac{1}{2} = \tfrac{7}{2} = 3\tfrac{1}{2}$, $73 \times \tfrac{1}{2} = \tfrac{73}{2} = 36\tfrac{1}{2}$, etc.

$1 \times 1\tfrac{1}{2} = 1 \times \tfrac{3}{2} = \tfrac{3}{2} = 1\tfrac{1}{2}$, $2 \times 1\tfrac{1}{2} = 2 \times \tfrac{3}{2} = \tfrac{6}{2} = 3$, $3 \times 1\tfrac{1}{2} = 3 \times \tfrac{3}{2} = \tfrac{9}{2} = 4\tfrac{1}{2}$, etc. (or $3 \times 1 = 3$, $3 \times \tfrac{1}{2} = 1\tfrac{1}{2}$, $3 \times 1\tfrac{1}{2} = 4\tfrac{1}{2}$).

$6 \times 15\tfrac{1}{2} = 6 \times 15 + 6 \times \tfrac{1}{2}$, etc.

$9 \times 80\tfrac{1}{2} = 9 \times 80 + 9 \times \tfrac{1}{2}$.

As $\tfrac{1}{2} \times 1 = \tfrac{1}{2}$, $\tfrac{1}{2} \times 6 = \tfrac{6}{2} = 3$, $\tfrac{1}{2} \times 9 = \tfrac{9}{2} = 4\tfrac{1}{2}$.

SUBTRACTION.

$1 - \frac{1}{2} = \frac{1}{2}$, $2 - \frac{1}{2} = 1\frac{1}{2}$ (for $2 - 1 = 1$; $1 - \frac{1}{2} = \frac{1}{2}$, $1 + \frac{1}{2} = 1\frac{1}{2}$), $3 - \frac{1}{2} = 2\frac{1}{2}$, $2 - 1\frac{1}{2} = \frac{1}{2}$ (for $2 - 1 = 1$; $1 - \frac{1}{2} = \frac{1}{2}$, $1 + \frac{1}{2} = 1\frac{1}{2}$), $6 - 4\frac{1}{2} = 1\frac{1}{2}$ (for $6 - 4 = 2$, $2 - \frac{1}{2} = 1\frac{1}{2}$), $9 - 3\frac{1}{2} = 5\frac{1}{2}$, etc. $2\frac{1}{2} - 1 = 1\frac{1}{2}$, $6\frac{1}{2} - 3 = 3\frac{1}{2}$ ($= [6 - 3] + \frac{1}{2}$), etc. $3\frac{1}{2} - 2\frac{1}{2} = 1$ ($3 - 2 = 1$, $\frac{1}{2} - \frac{1}{2} = 0$; or $3\frac{1}{2} - 2 = 1\frac{1}{2}$, $1\frac{1}{2} - \frac{1}{2} = 1$). $8\frac{1}{2} - 4\frac{1}{2} = ?$

DIVISION.

$\frac{1}{2}$ in $1 = 2$ (for $1 = \frac{2}{2}$ and $\frac{1}{2}$ in $\frac{2}{2} = 2$), $\frac{1}{2}$ in $4 = 8$ (for $4 = \frac{8}{2}$ and $\frac{1}{2}$ in $\frac{8}{2} = 8$; or $\frac{1}{2}$ in $1 = 2$ and $\frac{1}{2}$ in $4 = 4 \times 2$, or 8.) *

$1\frac{1}{2} \div \frac{1}{2} = \frac{3}{2} \div \frac{1}{2} = 3 \div 1 = 3$. †
$9\frac{1}{2} \div 1 = \frac{19}{2} \div \frac{2}{2}$, etc.
$6 \div 1\frac{1}{2} = \frac{12}{2} \div \frac{3}{2} = 12 \div 3 = 4$.
$10\frac{1}{2} \div 3\frac{1}{2} = \frac{21}{2} \div \frac{7}{2} = 21 \div 7 = 3$.

COMPARING.

½ *with* 1.

$\frac{1}{2} = 1 - \frac{1}{2}$, $1 = \frac{1}{2} + \frac{1}{2}$.
$\frac{1}{2} = $ the half of 1, $1 = $ two times $\frac{1}{2}$.
What number shows me the difference between $\frac{1}{2}$ and 1?
How much must I take from 16 to get $9\frac{1}{2}$?
One of two numbers is $9\frac{1}{2}$; the difference between it and a greater number is $6\frac{1}{2}$; what is the greater number?
Give two other numbers whose difference is $6\frac{1}{2}$, $4\frac{1}{2}$, $9\frac{1}{2}$.
How many times must I take $\frac{1}{2}$ to get 1? How many times $4\frac{1}{2}$ to get 9?
Of what number is $4\frac{1}{2}$ the half?
Of what number is 9 the double?
The divisor is $4\frac{1}{2}$, the quotient 2, what is the dividend?
What number must I take $\frac{1}{2}$ times to get $4\frac{1}{2}$?

---

* Though we indicate the division by the American method, the expression must not be read "1½ divided by ½," but "½ in 1½," or "½ contained in 1½." See page 156.

† We simply state the fact here and the reason therefor, leaving the teacher to choose the method of questioning. The method employed in the whole number can be applied here very well. For example :
How many halves in 1?
How many halves in 3?
How many halves in 2½?

APPLIED NUMBER.

What is $\frac{1}{2}$ a dollar? ($\frac{1}{2}$ a dollar equals one of two equal parts into which I divide a dollar.)

How many half dollars in 17 dimes? ($\frac{1}{2}$ dollar = 5 dimes, 17 dimes ÷ 5 dimes = 3 [2 dimes].)

In a hotel $17\frac{1}{2} + 13\frac{1}{2} + 8\frac{1}{2}$ pounds of meat were bought. How many "portions" will this make, allowing $\frac{1}{2}$ lb. to a portion?

SECOND STEP.
Thirds.
1.

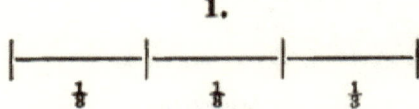

If I divide 1 into 3 equal parts, one part is $\frac{1}{3}$.

$\frac{1}{3}$ is one of the 3 equal parts into which I have divided 1.

$\frac{2}{3}$ are 2 of the 3 equal parts into which I have divided 1.

$$3 \text{ in } 1 = \frac{1}{3}, \text{ or } \frac{1}{3} \times 1 = \frac{1}{3}.$$

a. $\frac{1}{3} + \frac{1}{3} = \frac{2}{3}, \frac{2}{3} + \frac{1}{3} = \frac{3}{3} = 1.$

b. $1 \times \frac{1}{3} = \frac{1}{3}, 2 \times \frac{1}{3} = \frac{2}{3}, 3 \times \frac{1}{3} = \frac{3}{3} = 1.$

c. $1 - \frac{1}{3} = \frac{2}{3}, \frac{2}{3} - \frac{1}{3} = \frac{1}{3}.$

d. 3 in 1, or $1 \div 3 = \frac{1}{3}, 2 \div 3 = \frac{2}{3}, \frac{1}{3} + \frac{2}{3} = 1.$

$1 \div 3 = \frac{1}{3}, 2 \div 3 = \frac{2}{3}, 10 \div 3 = \frac{10}{3}.$

ADDITION.

$2 + \frac{1}{3} = 2\frac{1}{3}, 8 + 4\frac{1}{3} = 12\frac{1}{3}, 5\frac{1}{3} + 4\frac{1}{3} = 9\frac{2}{3}, 17\frac{2}{3} + 17\frac{1}{3} = 35,$
$17\frac{2}{3} + 17\frac{2}{3} = 35\frac{1}{3},$ etc.

MULTIPLICATION.

$1 \times \frac{1}{3} = \frac{1}{3}, 9 \times \frac{1}{3} = \frac{9}{3} = 3, 14 \times \frac{1}{3} = \frac{14}{3} = 4\frac{2}{3},$ etc.

$1 \times \frac{2}{3} = \frac{2}{3}, 9 \times \frac{2}{3} = \frac{18}{3} = 6, 14 \times \frac{2}{3} = \frac{28}{3} = 9\frac{1}{3}, 10 \times \frac{2}{3} = \frac{20}{3} = 6\frac{2}{3},$ etc.

$3 \times 1\frac{1}{3} = 4$ $(3 \times 1 + 3 \times \frac{1}{3},$ or $3 \times 1\frac{1}{3} = 3 \times \frac{4}{3} = \frac{12}{3} = 4),$
$9 \times 1\frac{1}{3} = 12,$ etc.

$3 \times 1\frac{2}{3} = 5, 5 \times 1\frac{2}{3} = 8\frac{1}{3}.$

As $\frac{1}{3} \times 1 = \frac{1}{3}, \frac{1}{3} \times 2 = \frac{2}{3}, \frac{1}{3} \times 6 = \frac{6}{3} = 2, \frac{1}{3} \times 7 = \frac{7}{3} = 2\frac{1}{3},$ etc.

$\frac{2}{3} \times 1 = \frac{2}{3}, \frac{2}{3} \times 2 = \frac{4}{3} = 1\frac{1}{3}, \frac{2}{3} \times 9 = \frac{18}{3} = 6, \frac{2}{3} \times 11 = \frac{22}{3} = 7\frac{1}{3},$ etc.

SUBTRACTION.

$1 - \frac{1}{8} = \frac{7}{8}$, $2 - \frac{1}{8} = 1\frac{7}{8}$, etc.

$1 - \frac{3}{8} = \frac{5}{8}$, $2 - \frac{3}{8} = 1\frac{5}{8}$, etc.

$2 - 1\frac{1}{8} = \frac{7}{8}$, $4 - 1\frac{1}{8} = 2\frac{7}{8}$, etc.

$7\frac{3}{8} - 4\frac{1}{8} = 3\frac{2}{8}$.

$7\frac{1}{8} - 4\frac{3}{8} = 2\frac{6}{8}$ $(7 - 4\frac{3}{8}) + \frac{1}{8}$, or $7\frac{1}{8} - 4 - \frac{3}{8}$.

DIVISION.

$\frac{1}{8}$ in $1 = 3$, $\frac{1}{8}$ in $2 = 2 \times 3 = 6$, $\frac{1}{8}$ in $3 = 3 \times 3 = 9$, etc.

$\frac{1}{8}$ in $14 = 42$ ($\frac{1}{8}$ in $1 = 3$, $14 \times 3 = 42$).

$\frac{2}{8}$ in $1 = \frac{3}{2}$ ($\frac{1}{8}$ in $1 = 3$, $\frac{2}{8}$ in $1 =$ one half of $3 = \frac{3}{2}$).

$6 \div \frac{2}{8} = 9$ ($6 \div \frac{1}{8} = 18$, $6 \div \frac{2}{8} = \frac{18}{2} = 9$).

$4\frac{2}{8} \div 2\frac{1}{8} = 2$ ($\frac{14}{3} \div \frac{7}{3} = 14 \div 7 = 2$).

$20 \div 6\frac{2}{8} = \frac{60}{3} \div \frac{20}{3} = 60 \div 20 = 3$.

COMPARING.

⅛ *with* 1.

$\frac{1}{8} = 1 - \frac{7}{8}$, $1 = \frac{1}{8} + \frac{7}{8}$.

$\frac{1}{8} = \frac{1}{8} \times 1$, $1 = 3 \times \frac{1}{3}$.

⅜ *with* 1.

$\frac{3}{8} = 1 - \frac{5}{8}$, $1 = 1 \times \frac{3}{8} + \frac{5}{8}$.

⅙ *with* ⅓.

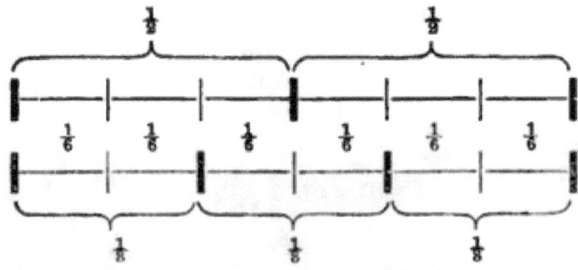

Thirds and halves **are** common (have a common de-nominator) in sixths.

$\frac{1}{2} = \frac{3}{6}$, $\frac{1}{3} = \frac{2}{6}$.

$\frac{1}{2} = \frac{1}{6} + \frac{1}{3}$, $\frac{1}{3} = \frac{1}{6} + \frac{1}{6}$.

$\frac{1}{3} = \frac{2}{3} \times \frac{1}{2}$ (twice the third part of $\frac{1}{2}$), for $\frac{1}{2}$ or $\frac{3}{6}$ in $\frac{1}{3}$ or $\frac{2}{6}$ ($= 3$ in 2) $\frac{2}{3}$ times.

$\frac{1}{2} = \frac{3}{2} \times \frac{1}{3}$ (3 times the half of $\frac{1}{3}$), for $\frac{1}{2} \div \frac{1}{3} = \frac{3}{6} \div \frac{2}{6} = 3 \div 2 = \frac{3}{2} = 1\frac{1}{2}$.

½ *with* ⅜.

$\frac{1}{2} = \frac{3}{6}$, $\frac{3}{8} = \frac{4}{6}$.

$\frac{1}{2} = \frac{3}{8} - \frac{1}{8}$, $\frac{3}{8} = \frac{1}{2} + \frac{2}{8}$.

$\frac{3}{8}$ into $\frac{1}{2} = \frac{4}{3}$, for $\frac{3}{8}$ into $\frac{1}{2} = 4$ into $3 = \frac{3}{4}$.

$\frac{3}{8} = \frac{4}{3} \times \frac{1}{2}$, for $\frac{1}{2}$ into $\frac{3}{8} = 3$ into $4 = \frac{4}{3}$.*

3 *with* 2.

3 is 1 greater than 2; 1 is ½ of 2; therefore 3 is ½ greater than 2. (Remark, ½ of 2 greater; the pupil is to learn that ½ does not always mean a part of a unit,—it may be a part of a whole number.)

If a boy has a string 3 yards long, it is ½ longer than a string 2 yards long.

3 hundred dollars is ½ more than 2 hundred dollars, 3 thousand dollars than 2 thousand dollars, etc.

Three is therefore one half greater than two.

2 is 1 less than 3. 1 is ⅓ of 3. 2 is therefore ⅓ less than 3. (Remark, ⅓ of 3 less; see remark above.)

If Henry has a string 2 yards long and Peter one 3 yards long, Henry's is ⅓ shorter than Peter's. (See remark above.)

If I have $200, I have ⅓ less than a man who has $300.

Two is one third of 3 less than three.

Give further examples.

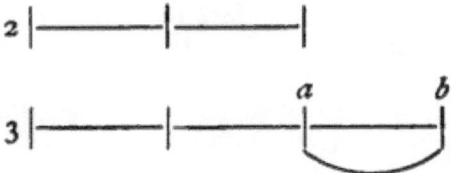

The first line indicates $2 \times 1 = 2$, the second $3 \times 1 = 3$; $a\,b$, the part of 3 greater than 2. The part $a\,b$ is ½ of 2; it equals also ⅓ of 3.

That is, the three has 3 of the same parts of which the two has only 2.

---

* The teacher must not forget that this work is chiefly mental, and does not need the use of slate. The above diagram, which appeals to the eye, will remove all seeming difficulties.

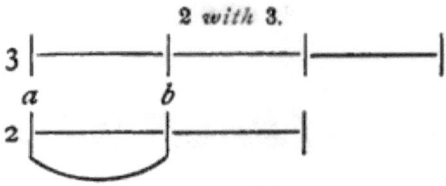

The two $= 2 \times \frac{1}{3}$ of $3 = \frac{2}{3} \times 3$.
The three $= 3 \times \frac{1}{2}$ of $2 = \frac{3}{2} \times 2$.

What is the relation of \$3 to \$2?
(\$3 $= \frac{3}{2}$ of \$2, \$2 $= \frac{2}{3}$ of \$3.)
What part of a yard are 2 feet?

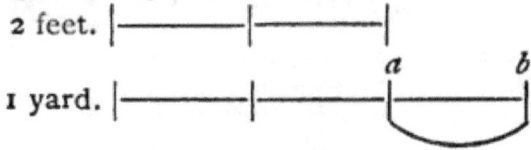

2 feet $= \frac{2}{3}$ of 1 yard.
1 yard $= \frac{3}{2}$ of 2 feet.

How many times is $\frac{1}{4} - \frac{1}{8}$ contained in 1? 2? 3?
How many times is $\frac{1}{4} - \frac{1}{8}$ contained in $\frac{5}{8}$?
How many times must I take $\frac{1}{8}$ to get 8?
$8 \times \frac{1}{4}$ is how much more than $8 \times \frac{1}{8}$? How much less than $8 \times \frac{3}{8}$?

How much is $\frac{2}{3}$ of 100 lbs.?
How many pounds more in $\frac{2}{3}$ than $\frac{1}{2}$ of 100 lbs.?
($\frac{1}{3}$ of 100 lbs. $= 33\frac{1}{3}$ lbs.; $\frac{2}{3} = 66\frac{2}{3}$ lbs.; $\frac{1}{2}$ of 100 lbs. $= 50$ lbs. $66\frac{2}{3}$ lbs. $- 50$ lbs. $= 16\frac{2}{3}$ lbs.)

How many packages of tea, each weighing $\frac{1}{4}$ lb., can be made from 15 lbs.? $\frac{1}{8}$ lb. packages?

THIRD STEP.

Fourths.

1.

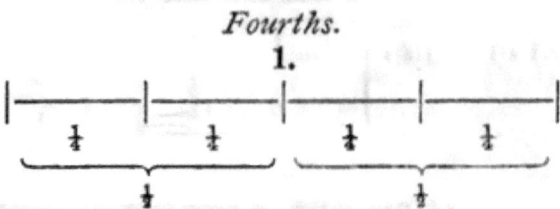

If I divide 1 into 4 equal parts, one part $= \frac{1}{4}$.   4 in 1 $=$ $\frac{1}{4}$, $\frac{1}{4} \times 1 = \frac{1}{4}$.

ADDITION.

$$\tfrac{1}{4} + \tfrac{1}{4} = \tfrac{2}{4} = \tfrac{1}{2}, \quad \tfrac{2}{4} + \tfrac{1}{4} = \tfrac{3}{4}, \quad \tfrac{3}{4} + \tfrac{1}{4} = \tfrac{4}{4} = \tfrac{2}{2} = 1.$$

MULTIPLICATION.

$$1 \times \tfrac{1}{4} = \tfrac{1}{4}, \quad 2 \times \tfrac{1}{4} = \tfrac{2}{4} = \tfrac{1}{2}, \quad 3 \times \tfrac{1}{4} = \tfrac{3}{4}, \quad 4 \times \tfrac{1}{4} = \tfrac{4}{4} = 1.$$

SUBTRACTION.

$$1 - \tfrac{1}{4} = \tfrac{3}{4}, \quad \tfrac{3}{4} - \tfrac{1}{4} = \tfrac{2}{4} = \tfrac{1}{2}, \quad \tfrac{2}{4} - \tfrac{1}{4} = \tfrac{1}{4}.$$

DIVISION.

$$\tfrac{1}{4} \text{ in } \tfrac{1}{4} = 1, \quad \tfrac{1}{4} \text{ in } \tfrac{1}{2} = 2, \quad \tfrac{1}{4} \text{ in } \tfrac{3}{4} = 3, \quad \tfrac{1}{4} \text{ in } 1 = 4.$$
$$1 \div 4 = \tfrac{1}{4}, \quad 2 \div 4 = \tfrac{2}{4} = \tfrac{1}{2}, \quad 3 \div 4 = \tfrac{3}{4}.$$

MIXED.

$4\tfrac{1}{4} + \tfrac{3}{4} = 4 + \tfrac{4}{4} = 4 + 1 = 5.$

$4\tfrac{1}{2} + 4\tfrac{1}{4} = 8\tfrac{3}{4}$, etc.

$1 \times \tfrac{1}{4} = \tfrac{1}{4}, \quad 9 \times \tfrac{1}{4} = \tfrac{9}{4} = 2\tfrac{1}{4}.$

$9 \times 1\tfrac{1}{4} = 9 + \tfrac{9}{4} = 9 + 2 + \tfrac{1}{4} = 11\tfrac{1}{4}.$

$9 \times 3\tfrac{3}{4} = 27 + \tfrac{27}{4} = 27 + 6\tfrac{3}{4} = 33\tfrac{3}{4}.$

$\tfrac{1}{4} \times 9 = \tfrac{9}{4}, \quad \tfrac{3}{4} \times 9 = \tfrac{27}{4}, \quad \tfrac{3}{4} \times 16 = \tfrac{48}{4} = 12.$

$1 - \tfrac{1}{4} = \tfrac{3}{4}, \quad 16 - \tfrac{1}{4} = 15\tfrac{3}{4}.$

$20 - \tfrac{3}{4} = 19\tfrac{1}{4}, \quad 20\tfrac{3}{4} - \tfrac{1}{2} = 20\tfrac{1}{4}.$

$20 - 6\tfrac{3}{4} = 13\tfrac{1}{4}, \quad 20\tfrac{3}{4} - 6\tfrac{1}{2} = 14\tfrac{1}{4}.$

$1 \div \tfrac{1}{4} = 4, \quad 8 \div \tfrac{1}{4} = 8 \times 4 = 32, \quad 32 \div \tfrac{1}{4} = 4 \times 32 = 128.$

$5 \div \tfrac{1}{4} = \tfrac{20}{4} \div \tfrac{1}{4} = 20 \div 1 = 20.$

$5\tfrac{3}{4} \div \tfrac{1}{4} = \tfrac{23}{4} \div \tfrac{1}{4} = 23 \div 1 = 23.$

$25 \div 6\tfrac{1}{4} = 4 \ (25 = \tfrac{100}{4}, \ 6\tfrac{1}{4} = \tfrac{25}{4}).$

$27 \times 4 \div 6\tfrac{3}{4} \ (1 \div \tfrac{1}{4} = 4, \ 27 \div \tfrac{27}{4} = 27).$

$1 \div \tfrac{3}{4} = \tfrac{4}{3} = 1\tfrac{1}{3} \ (\tfrac{1}{4} + \tfrac{3}{4} = 4 \div 3 = \tfrac{4}{3} = 1\tfrac{1}{3}).$

$2, \ 3, \ 4, \ 5, \ 6 \div \tfrac{3}{4}.$

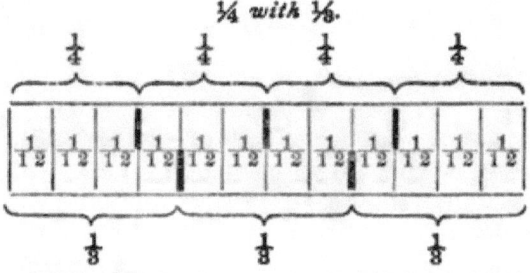

¼ with ⅓

Fourths and thirds have a common denominator in twelve.

$\frac{1}{4} = \frac{3}{12}$, $\frac{1}{3} = \frac{4}{12}$.

$\frac{1}{4} = \frac{1}{3} - \frac{1}{12}$, $\frac{1}{3} = \frac{1}{4} + \frac{1}{12}$.

$\frac{1}{4} = \frac{3}{4} \times \frac{1}{3}$, for $\frac{1}{4} \div \frac{1}{3} = \frac{3}{4}$ $(\frac{3}{12} \div \frac{4}{12})$.

$\frac{1}{3} = \frac{4}{3} \times \frac{1}{4}$, for $\frac{1}{3} \div \frac{1}{4} = \frac{4}{3}$ $(\frac{4}{12} \div \frac{3}{12})$

¼ with ⅜.

$\frac{1}{4} = \frac{3}{12}$, $\frac{3}{8} = \frac{8}{12}$.

$\frac{1}{4} = \frac{3}{8} - \frac{5}{12}$, $\frac{3}{8} = \frac{1}{4} + \frac{5}{12}$.

$\frac{1}{4} = \frac{2}{3} \times \frac{3}{8}$ ($\frac{1}{3}$ of $\frac{3}{8}$ taken 3 times), for $\frac{1}{4} \div \frac{3}{8} = \frac{2}{3}$.

$\frac{3}{8} = \frac{3}{2} \times \frac{1}{4}$, for $\frac{3}{8} \div \frac{1}{4}$ $(\frac{9}{12} \div \frac{3}{12})$.

¾ with ⅜.

$\frac{3}{4} = \frac{9}{12}$, $\frac{3}{8} = \frac{8}{12}$.

$\frac{3}{4} = \frac{3}{8} + \frac{1}{12}$, $\frac{3}{8} = \frac{3}{4} - \frac{1}{12}$.

$\frac{3}{4} = \frac{9}{8} \times \frac{3}{8}$, for $\frac{3}{4} \div \frac{3}{8} = \frac{9}{8} = 1\frac{1}{8}$.

$\frac{3}{8} = \frac{8}{9} \times \frac{3}{4}$, for $\frac{3}{8} \div \frac{3}{4} = \frac{8}{9}$ $(\frac{8}{12} \div \frac{9}{12})$.

What is the common denominator of halves, thirds, and fourths?

$1 = \frac{12}{12}$, $\frac{1}{2} \times \frac{12}{12} = \frac{6}{12}$, $\frac{1}{3} \times \frac{12}{12} = \frac{4}{12}$, $\frac{1}{4} \times \frac{12}{12} = \frac{3}{12}$.

What relation do the numbers 3 and 4 bear to each other?

$3 = 3 \times 1$, $4 = 4 \times 1$. $1 = \frac{1}{4} \times 4$, $3 = \frac{3}{4} \times 4$. $1 = \frac{1}{3} \times 3$, $4 = \frac{4}{3} \times 3$. 4 is $\frac{1}{3}$ times greater than 3, and 3 is $\frac{1}{4}$ times smaller than 4.

Show the same relation with 3, 6, 9, 10 times 3 and 4.

Two numbers have a sum of $16\frac{5}{12}$; one is $6\frac{2}{3}$. What is the other?

$(16\frac{5}{12} - 6\frac{2}{3} = 16 - 6\frac{2}{3} + \frac{5}{12}$. $16 - 6 = 10$, $10 - \frac{2}{3} = 9\frac{1}{3}$ $+ \frac{5}{12} = 9\frac{9}{12} = 9\frac{3}{4}$.)

The difference between $16\frac{5}{12}$ and an unknown number is $9\frac{3}{4}$.

What is the unknown number?

$(16\frac{5}{12} - 9\frac{3}{4} = 16 - 9\frac{3}{4} + \frac{5}{12}$.)

Suppose $16\frac{5}{12}$ to be the smaller number, and the difference $9\frac{3}{4}$; what is the larger number?

$(16\frac{5}{12} + 9\frac{3}{4} = 16\frac{5}{12} + \frac{9}{12} + 9$.)

What is the relation of 1 cwt. to $\frac{3}{4}$ cwt. in whole numbers?

How many times must I take $\frac{3}{4}$ cwt. in order to get 1 cwt.?

(As the relation of $\frac{3}{4}$ cwt. to 1 cwt. is as 3 to 4, I must take 4 times $\frac{1}{3}$, or $\frac{4}{3}$ of $\frac{3}{4}$ cwt.)

How many times must I take $6\frac{1}{4}$ to get $8\frac{1}{3}$?

(As often as $6\frac{1}{4}$ is contained in $8\frac{1}{3}$. $6\frac{1}{4} = \frac{25}{4}$; $8\frac{1}{3} = \frac{25}{3}$; $\frac{25}{3} \div \frac{25}{4} = \frac{1}{3} \div \frac{1}{4} = \frac{4}{3}$.)

How many times must I take $8\frac{1}{3}$ to get $6\frac{1}{4}$?

(As many times as $8\frac{1}{3}$ is contained in $6\frac{1}{4}$, etc.)

$\frac{1}{3}$ of $6\frac{1}{4}$ is $\frac{1}{4}$ of what number?

$\frac{1}{4}$ of $8\frac{1}{3}$ is what part of $6\frac{1}{4}$?

If I take 12 from a number and still have $\frac{1}{4}$ of the number left, what is the number?

(Since I still have $\frac{1}{4}$, I must have taken $\frac{3}{4}$ away; so 12 $= \frac{3}{4}$ of the unknown number, and $\frac{4}{4}$ or the whole equals 4 times $\frac{1}{3}$ of 12 or 16.)

What is the relation of the 12 to the whole number?

What is the relation of the remainder to the subtrahend?

How many pounds in $\frac{3}{4}$ cwt.?

How many oz. in $\frac{3}{4}$ lb.?

How many pwt. in $\frac{3}{4}$ oz.?

How much more is $\frac{1}{2} + \frac{1}{6} + \frac{1}{4}$ of a dollar than $\frac{3}{4}$ of a dollar?

N had \$100 to spend in travel. How long can he travel if he spend $1\frac{1}{4}$ dollars per day?

(He can travel as many days as $1\frac{1}{4}$ dollars are contained in 100 dollars. $1\frac{1}{4} = \frac{5}{4}$. $\frac{1}{4}$ in 100 $= 400$; $\frac{5}{4} = \frac{1}{5}$ of \$400 or \$80. Or \$100 $\div \frac{5}{4} = $ \$80.)

N was $2\frac{2}{3}$ months on a journey and spent \$100. How much did he spend per day?

N was $2\frac{2}{3}$ months on a journey, spending $1\frac{1}{4}$ dollars a day. How much did his journey cost him?

A and B gave a poor family some money. A gave \$36 more than B, who gave only $\frac{3}{4}$ as much as A. How much money did each give, and how much did both give?

CONSIDERATION.

Compare A's gift with B's.

A's gift = B's gift + \$36.
B's gift = $\frac{3}{4}$ × A's gift.

If B gave $\frac{3}{4}$ as much as A, the latter gave $\frac{4}{4}$.

How many parts did A give, and how many B? A gave 4 and B 3 parts.   Both gave 4 + 3 = 7 parts.

How many more parts did A give than B?

What is one part of the whole?   ($\frac{1}{7}$.)

How many dollars did A give more than B?

Then \$36 = what part of the whole?   ($\frac{1}{7}$.)

Since \$36 = $\frac{1}{7}$, how much is the whole or $\frac{7}{7}$?

($7 \times \$36 = \$252$.)

What part of this did A give, and what part B?

A and B gave together \$252, of which A gave \$144; how much did B give?

B gave \$108; how much did A give?

A gave \$144, B \$36 less.

That which A gave more than B was $\frac{1}{7}$ of the whole; what was the whole?

FOURTH STEP.

Fifths.

1.

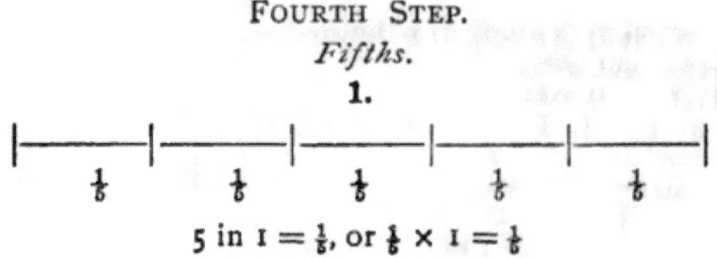

5 in $1 = \frac{1}{5}$, or $\frac{1}{5} \times 1 = \frac{1}{5}$

Proceed as in the former steps.

COMPARING.

a. $\frac{1}{5}$ *with* $\frac{1}{4}$.

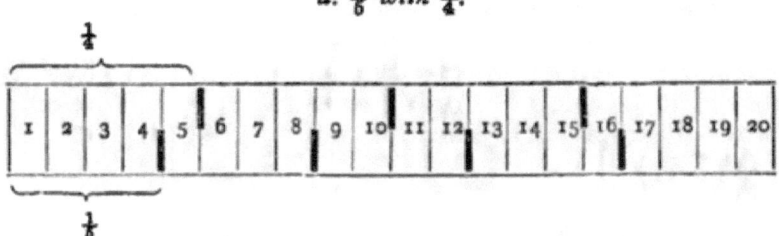

Compare $\frac{1}{5}$ with $\frac{2}{4}$, $\frac{2}{5}$ with $\frac{1}{4}$, $\frac{3}{5}$ with $\frac{2}{4}$.

(Allow the pupils to illustrate these comparisons on the blackboard.)

b. $\frac{1}{6}$ *with* $\frac{1}{5}$.

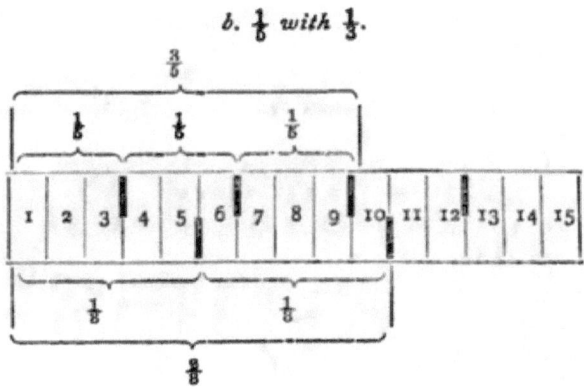

Compare $\frac{3}{5}$ with $\frac{3}{5}$.

$$\frac{3}{5} = \frac{9}{15}, \frac{3}{5} = \frac{10}{15}, \frac{3}{5} = \frac{3}{5} - \frac{1}{15}$$
etc.

c. What is the common denominator of halves, thirds, fourths, and fifths?

(Halves, thirds, and fourths have a common denominator in 12. If I divide 12 by fifths or 5 by twelfths, I get sixtieths. So $\frac{1}{2} = \frac{30}{60}, \frac{1}{3} = \frac{20}{60}, \frac{1}{4} = \frac{15}{60}, \frac{1}{5} = \frac{15}{60}$.

d. Since $\frac{1}{4} + \frac{1}{6} = \frac{5}{4}$, $6 \times \frac{1}{4} \div 6 \times \frac{1}{6} = 1\frac{2}{4} \div 1\frac{1}{6} = \frac{5}{4}$; $10 \times \frac{1}{4} \div 10 \times \frac{1}{6} = 2\frac{2}{4} \div 2 = \frac{5}{4}$.

Since $\frac{2}{5} + \frac{3}{5} = \frac{3}{5}$, $3 \times \frac{2}{5} \div 3 \times \frac{3}{5} = \frac{3}{5}$; $9 = \frac{2}{5} \div 9 \times \frac{3}{5} = \frac{3}{5}$.

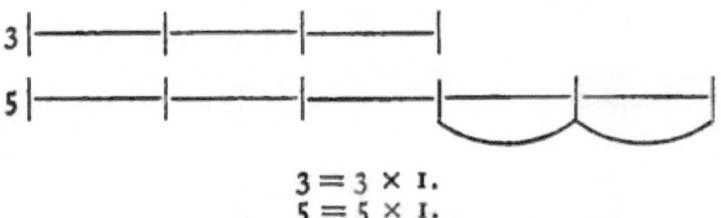

$$3 = 3 \times 1.$$
$$5 = 5 \times 1.$$

As $1 = \frac{1}{5}$ of 5, 3 is $\frac{2}{5} \times 5$ less than 5.
As $1 = \frac{1}{3}$ of 3, 5 is $\frac{2}{3}$ greater than 3.

The 5 has 5 of the same kind of parts of which the 3 has 3; therefore $5 = \frac{5}{3} \times 3$ and $3 = \frac{3}{5} \times 5$.

The relation occurs with 6 and 10 (2×3 and 2×5), 9 and 15, 12 and 20, etc.

In the same manner find the relation of 4 and 5, and their multiples.

1 dozen = $\frac{4}{5}$ of 15, 15 = $\frac{5}{4}$ of 1 dozen.

e. Two numbers, of which one is $6\frac{1}{5}$, have a sum of $18\frac{2}{3}$. What is the other number?

($18\frac{2}{3} - 6\frac{1}{5}$. $18 - 6 = 12$, $\frac{2}{3} - \frac{1}{5} = \frac{10}{15} - \frac{3}{15} = \frac{7}{15}$. $18\frac{2}{3} - 6\frac{1}{5} = 12\frac{7}{15}$.   Or: $18\frac{2}{3} - 6 = 12\frac{2}{3}$, $12\frac{2}{3} - \frac{1}{5} = 12\frac{10}{15} - \frac{3}{15} = 12\frac{7}{15}$.   Or: $18\frac{2}{3} - 6\frac{1}{5} = 18 - 6\frac{1}{5} + \frac{2}{3}$. $18 - 6\frac{1}{5} = 11\frac{4}{5} + \frac{2}{3} = 11\frac{12}{15} + \frac{10}{15} = 12\frac{7}{15}$.)

f. How many times must I take $3\frac{3}{5}$ to get 18?

($3\frac{3}{5} = \frac{18}{5}$, $18 = \frac{90}{5}$; $\frac{18}{5}$ in $\frac{90}{5} = 18$ in $90 = 5$.)

3. How do I get $\frac{4}{5}$ of a cwt.?

($\frac{1}{5}$ of 1 cwt. taken 4 times.)

Express the difference between $\frac{1}{2}$ cwt. and $\frac{1}{3}$ cwt. in pounds. $\frac{1}{2}$ and $\frac{1}{4}$. $\frac{1}{3}$ and $\frac{1}{4}$. $\frac{1}{4}$ and $\frac{1}{5}$. $\frac{1}{4}$ and $\frac{1}{8}$, etc.

How many dimes must I add to $\frac{1}{2}$ of a dollar to get $\frac{4}{5}$ of a dollar?

If $\frac{1}{3}$ lb. costs $\frac{1}{4}$ dollar, how much will $\frac{1}{9}$ lb. cost?

(Since $\frac{1}{3}$ lb. costs $\frac{1}{4}$ dollar, 1 lb. will cost $3 \times \frac{1}{4} = \frac{3}{4}$ dollar. $\frac{1}{9}$ lb. will cost then $\frac{1}{9} \times \frac{3}{4}$ dollar $= \frac{3}{20}$ dollar.

If a man applies $\frac{2}{3}$ of his income for his support, $\frac{1}{5}$ of the remainder for pleasure, and has $48 left, how much is his income?

(As he spends $\frac{2}{3}$ for his support, there remains $\frac{1}{3}$. He spends $\frac{1}{5}$ of the remainder $[\frac{1}{5} \times \frac{1}{3}]$ $\frac{1}{15}$ for pleasure. Thus he spends $\frac{2}{3} + \frac{1}{15} = \frac{10}{15} + \frac{1}{15} = \frac{11}{15}$, and retains $\frac{4}{15}$. Then $\frac{4}{15} = \$48$, $\frac{1}{15} = \$12$ and $\frac{15}{15} = \$180$.)

How much money does his support cost him? His pleasure how much? What relation do these amounts bear to each other? What relation between the money for pleasure and that spared? What part of the whole is the $48?

A person has an income of $180. He spends $\frac{2}{3}$ for his support and $\frac{1}{15}$ for pleasure. How much does he save?

A man has an income of $180, $\frac{2}{3}$ of which is necessary for his support, and $48 is saved. How much and what part does he spend for pleasure?

FIFTH STEP.

Sixths.

1.

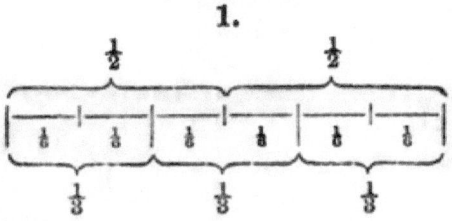

As in preceding steps :

$\frac{1}{6} + \frac{1}{6} = \frac{1}{3}, \frac{1}{3} + \frac{1}{6} = \frac{1}{2}, \frac{1}{2} + \frac{1}{6} = \frac{2}{3}, \frac{2}{3} + \frac{1}{6} = \frac{5}{6}, \frac{5}{6} + \frac{1}{6} = 1.$

$1 \times \frac{1}{6} = \frac{1}{6}, 2 \times \frac{1}{6} = \frac{1}{3}, 3 \times \frac{1}{6} = \frac{1}{2},$ etc.

$1 - \frac{1}{6} = \frac{5}{6}, \frac{5}{6} - \frac{1}{6} = \frac{4}{6} = \frac{2}{3}, \frac{2}{3} - \frac{1}{6} = \frac{3}{6} = \frac{1}{2}, \frac{1}{2} - \frac{1}{6} = \frac{1}{3},$ etc.

$1 \div \frac{1}{6} = 6, 1 \div \frac{2}{6} = 3, 1 \div \frac{3}{6} = 2,$ etc.

a. As 6 parts = 2 × 3 or 3 × 2 parts, sixths can be expressed in thirds and halves. As 8 parts = 2 × 4 or 4 × 2 parts, eighths can be expressed in halves and fourths. In the same way twelfths can be reduced to halves, thirds, fourths, and sixths.

Why cannot $\frac{1}{5}$ be expressed in halves or thirds? (Because $\frac{1}{5}$ is not contained in $\frac{5}{6}$ without remainder.)

b. Compare $\frac{1}{8}$ and $\frac{1}{6}$.

(Pupil will now be able to do this without help.)

Compare $\frac{1}{8}$ with $\frac{1}{4}$?

(Pupil resolves both into 24ths, and soon sees that 12ths are still more simple.

c. What is the common denominator of halves, thirds, fourths, and sixths?

What is the difference between $\frac{4}{4}$ and $\frac{5}{6}$? $\frac{3}{4}$ and $\frac{5}{6}$?

What relation exists between 5 and 6?

$(5 = \frac{5}{6} \times 6, 6 = \frac{6}{5} \times 5.)$

Show that $\frac{1}{5}$ of 5 and $\frac{1}{5}$ of 6 hold the same relation as 5 and 6 do. Also that 2 times 5 and 2 times 6 hold the same relation that 5 and 6 do.

1 dime $= \frac{1}{10}$ of a dollar.
2 dimes $= \frac{2}{10} = \frac{1}{5}$ of a dollar.
3 dimes $= \frac{3}{10}$ of a dollar.
4 dimes $= \frac{4}{10} = \frac{2}{5}$ of a dollar.
etc.

$$1 \text{ oz.} = \tfrac{1}{16} \text{ of a pound.}$$
$$2 \text{ oz.} = \tfrac{2}{16} = \tfrac{1}{8} \text{ of a pound.}$$
$$3 \text{ oz.} = \tfrac{3}{16} \text{ of a pound.}$$
$$4 \text{ oz.} = \tfrac{4}{16} = \tfrac{1}{4} \text{ of a pound.}$$
etc.

In the same manner make practical applications of fractions in connection with compound numbers and in daily life. These five steps will be sufficient to illustrate the method. The teacher will easily lead the pupils step by step, until they are able to do the work alone. Many examples must be given in order that the pupils become thorough and efficient. This work will employ the first half of the year.

SECOND HALF OF THE YEAR.

THE FOUR FUNDAMENTAL RULES IN FRACTIONS.

The pupils have been thus far taught to consider the fraction from all sides. It remains now to take each operation by itself, and bring the knowledge of it to completion. Let it not be forgotten that accuracy and rapidity must be secured before the pupil can be said to have reached complete mastery of any step.

CLASSIFICATION.

1. Nature and manner of treating the fraction in general (explanation of the parts, kinds, etc., amplifying, common denominator, etc.)
2. Resolution (resolving).
3. Reduction.
4. Addition.
5. Subtraction.
6. Multiplication,
7. Division,

In abstract and concrete numbers oral and written,

There will be no difficulty in connection with these steps, if the preceding have been carefully taught.   Grube calls especial attention to the following points :

I. *The Unity.*

The pupil has already learned that when 1 is divided into 4 equal parts, one part = ¼.

Three fourths are 3 of the 4 parts, into which 1 has been divided.

The unity may be of any size or number which is divided into equal parts, as : a yard, a cwt., a ton, etc.

Draw ¼ of a yard, ¾ of a yard.

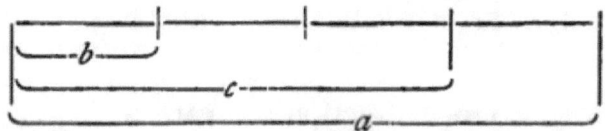

In order to get *b* what must I first have ?   (*a.*)

What is *a* ?   (The whole or unity.)

What quantity in the figure constitutes the unity ? (The yard.)

If we consider *a*, 1 cwt., as unity, how much does *b* equal ?   *c* ?   (¼ cwt., ¾ cwt.)

How many pounds would *b* equal ?   *c* ?

If *b* = 25 lbs., how much is the unity or whole ?

If *b* = 27½ lbs., how much is the unity ?

27½ lbs.

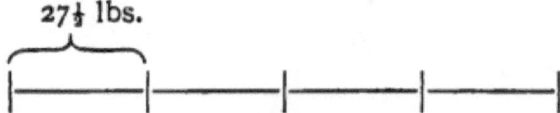

The number with which I indicate the unity is 1.

What do we call the numbers which indicate parts of the unity ?

What is ¼ ?   ¾ ?   ½ ?   (A fraction.)

What then is a fraction ?   (A fraction is one or more of the equal parts of a unity.)

How many parts have we in ¼ ?   (We have 1 part.)

In ¾ ?   (We have 3 parts.)

Into what is the unity divided when we get ⅓? (Into 3 parts or thirds.)

When we get ⅚? (Into 6 parts or sixths.)

What do we call the 6 or the number below the line? (The denominator.)

What do we call the 5 or the number above the line? (The numerator.)

The teacher must give many more questions similar to the above, until the pupils understand thoroughly the meaning of the terms *fraction, numerator,* and *denominator.*

How does the fraction ¾ compare with unity? (It is less than unity.)

The fraction ⅓? (It is less than unity.)

A fraction which is less than unity, we call a proper fraction.

How does a proper fraction compare with unity? (It is less.)

(Many more similar questions.)

What fraction equals the unit? (That which takes all the parts into which the unit is divided.)

Express the unity in thirds, fourths, tenths, thousandths.

(The transition from proper to improper fractions is easy.)

2. *Expansion and Reduction.*

If you multiply ¾ by 3, what do you get?
Illustrate this.

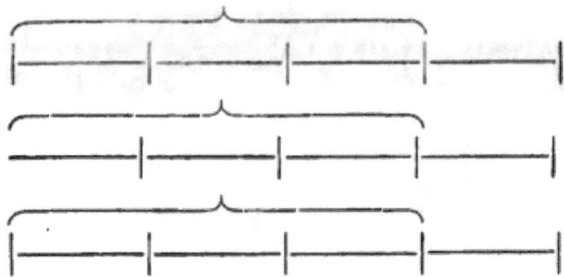

Change ¾ into whole numbers.

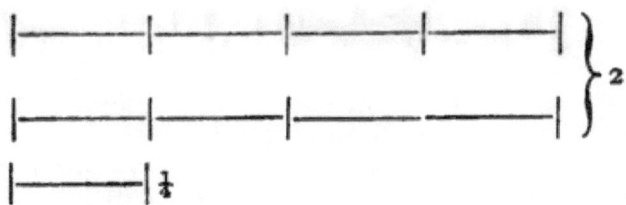

Which term of the fraction have I multiplied, and which remains unchanged in expanding ¾?

(Numerator has been multiplied, denominator unchanged.)

If I multiply the numerator by 3, 5, 10, etc., what of the value of the fraction?

(3, 5, 10, etc., times greater.)

Leaving the numerator unchanged and multiply the denominator by 3, what fraction do we get? ($\frac{3}{12}$.)

How does ¾ compare with $\frac{3}{12}$? (It is 3 times as large.)

If I multiply the denominator 4 by 3, it is the same as to take what part of the fraction?

Illustrate this.

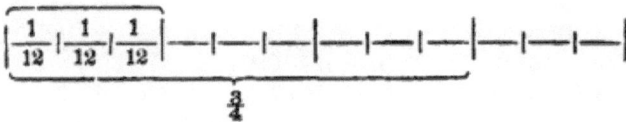

If ¾ be divided by 3 we get $\frac{3}{12} = \frac{1}{4}$.

What must be done with $\frac{3}{12}$ or ¼ to get again the first value or ¾?

What effect upon the value of a fraction if both numerator and denominator are multiplied by the same number?

Continue work of this kind until the pupils are familiar with all the changes, such as multiplying or dividing th numerator or denominator, or both, etc. Illustrate each step in the manner already indicated. This will include reducing to lower terms, to higher terms, to fractions having a given denominator, improper fractions to mixed numbers, mixed numbers to improper fractions, etc.

3. *Common Denominator.*

It is necessary in adding fractions to find a common denominator, that is, a general denominator into which the other denominators will go without a remainder. It must also the *smallest* number into which all the denominators will go without a remainder. This can be found by using the prime factors of the numbers whose common denominator we seek. Take $\frac{1}{4}$ and $\frac{1}{6}$.

$$4 = 2 \times 2$$
$$6 \times 3 \times 2$$

Both the 4 and 6 have the common factor 2, and this is taken but once. We then have $3 \times 2 \times 2 = 12$. Since the factors of 6 (3×2), and those of 4 (2×2) are found in the factors of 12 ($3 \times 2 \times 2$), 12 will contain 6 and 4, and is their common denominator—it is also the common denominator of $\frac{1}{4} = \frac{3}{12}$, and $\frac{1}{6} = \frac{2}{12}$.

Take $\frac{1}{15}$, $\frac{3}{18}$, $\frac{1}{9}$.

$$15 = 5 \times 3$$
$$18 = 2 \times 3 \times 3$$
$$9 = 3 \times 3$$

Since 9 is contained in 18, it is also contained in a multiple of 18. Therefore the common denominator of 15 and 18 will also contain 9; so we will consider 15 and 18.

15 and 18 have the common factor 3. In the factors $5 \times 3 \times 3 \times 2$ we find all the factors of 15 and 18; therefore their product, or 90, is a common dividend for both and also for 9.

Give other examples.

Add the following fractions:

$$\tfrac{25}{36} + \tfrac{13}{15} + \tfrac{4}{11} + \tfrac{8}{105} + \tfrac{1}{3}.$$

Write the denominators in a column, placing at the left a small prime factor which will be contained in two or more of them:

$$3 \left\{ \begin{array}{l} 36 = 12 \times 3 \\ 15 = 5 \times 3 \\ 11 = 11 \\ 105 = 35 \times 3 \\ 3 = 1 \times 3 \end{array} \right.$$

But there is another prime factor (5) which is contained in more than one of the numbers:

$$5 \begin{cases} 36 = 12 \times 3 \\ 15 = 3 \\ 11 = 11 \\ 105 = 35 = 7 \times 5 \\ 3 = 1 \times 3 \end{cases}$$

We have then remaining the factors 12, 3, 11, 7, 5.
Or it may be expressed in a shorter way :*

$$\begin{cases} 3 | 36, \ 15, \ 11, \ 105, \ 3 \\ \overline{5 | 12, \ \ 5, \ 11, \ \ 35, \ 1} \\ \overline{\ \ \ | 12, \ \ 1, \ 11, \ \ \ 7} \end{cases}$$

4. *Number Relations in the Fractional Form.*

What relations exists between the numbers 5 and 9?

If I wish to measure two numbers, I must measure them with one another by the same measure. But 5 and 9 have no common measure besides the 1. As $5 = 5 \times 1$, 1 must equal $\frac{1}{5} \times 5$ with reference to the 5, and $\frac{1}{9} \times 9$ with reference to the 9. Therefore 9 in relation to the 5 is nine times $\frac{1}{5}$ of 5, and 5 is five times $\frac{1}{9}$ of 9.

5 and 9.

$$\begin{array}{l|l} 5 = 5 \times 1 & 9 = 9 \times 1 \\ 1 = \frac{1}{5} \times 5 & 1 = \frac{1}{9} \times 9 \end{array}$$

It follows :

$$5 = \tfrac{5}{9} \times 9 \text{ and}$$
$$9 = \tfrac{9}{5} \times 5.$$

---

* To assist in factoring, notice the following facts :

1. All numbers which end in o are exactly divisible by 2 and 5.
2. All numbers which end in o or 5 are exactly divisible by 5.
3. All numbers which end in 2, 4, 6 or 8 are exactly divisible by 2.
4. All numbers are exactly divisible by 3, the sum of whose digits is divisible by 3. For example, 4365, the sum of the digits is 18; since 18 is divisible by 3, 4365 is also.
5. All numbers are exactly divisible by 9, the sum of whose digits is divisible by 9.
6. All numbers are divisible by 6 which are divisible by 2 and 3.
7. All numbers are divisible by 8, the sum of whose last three figures is divisible by 8.

3 and 4.

$$3 = \tfrac{3}{4} \times 4$$
$$4 = \tfrac{4}{3} \times 3.$$

In comparing 3 and 9 with 1 as the measure, I have $3 = \tfrac{3}{9} \times 9$, $9 = \tfrac{9}{3} \times 3$. With 3 as the measure, I have

$$3 = \tfrac{1}{3} \times 9$$
$$9 = 3 \times 3.$$

APPLICATION.

If 5 yards of cloth cost \$4, what will 9 yards cost?

(As 9 yards = $\tfrac{9}{5} \times$ 5 yards, they will cost $\tfrac{9}{5} \times$ \$4 = $\tfrac{36}{5}$ = \$7$\tfrac{1}{5}$.)

As every fraction is a division, and every example in proportion goes out from a divisor and dividend, it is advisable to make use (according to Grube's idea) of the fractional form of expression in proportion. It has the advantage that it shows objectively the solution of the example.

If 5 yards cost \$4, what will 9 yards cost?

(Suppose that 1 yard costs \$4, 9 yards will be worth 9 × \$4. It is not 1 yard, but 5 yards that cost \$4; therefore the price will be 5 times less.

$$\frac{9 \times 4}{5} \text{ dollars} = \frac{36}{5} = \$7\tfrac{1}{5}.)$$

A quantity of hay will last 5 horses 4 days; how long will it last 9 horses?

(Suppose the hay was sufficient for 1 horse for 4 days, for 9 horses it would last $\tfrac{4}{9}$ days. But as it is sufficient for 5 horses instead of 1, it will last 5 times $\tfrac{4}{9}$ days =

$$\frac{5 \times 4}{9} = \frac{20}{9} = 2\tfrac{2}{9} \text{ days.}$$

3$\tfrac{3}{4}$ bushels of rye cost \$5; what will 4 bushels cost at the same rate?

$$\frac{4 \times 5}{3\tfrac{3}{4}} \text{ dollars} = \frac{20}{3\tfrac{3}{4}} = \frac{4 \times 20}{15} = \frac{80}{15} = 5\tfrac{1}{3} \text{ dollars.}$$

4 bushels cost \$5, what will 3$\tfrac{3}{4}$ bushels cost?

$$\frac{5 \times 3\tfrac{3}{4}}{4} = \frac{5 \times \tfrac{15}{4}}{4} = \frac{5 \times 15}{4 \times 4} = \frac{75}{16} = 4\tfrac{11}{16} \text{ dollars.})$$

This method is more elementary than the usual method of stating proportion, and it is none the less a practice in thinking.

The elementary school has accomplished enough in the first four years, if it has brought the pupil to be able to solve simple practical examples rapidly and accurately either by analyzing back to unity, or by means of the fractional method, or by comparing the relations. He will also be able to decide by his own observation which method of solution is the best for any given example. A pupil, who knows 95 to equal 5×19 will easily solve such an example as the following: If $6\frac{1}{3}$ lbs. of flour cost 20 cents, what will 95 lbs. cost?

($6\frac{1}{3} = \frac{19}{3}$. As $95 = 5 \times 19$, 95 lbs. $= 15 \times \frac{19}{3}$ pounds. $\frac{19}{3}$ lbs. cost 20 c., and 15×20 c. $= 300$ c.

Analyzing back to unity:

$$6\frac{1}{3} \text{ lbs.} \ldots \ldots \ldots \ldots 20 \text{ c.}$$

$$\frac{1}{3} \text{ " } \ldots \ldots \ldots \ldots \frac{20}{19} \text{ c.}$$

$$1 \text{ " } \ldots \ldots \ldots \frac{60}{19} = 3\frac{3}{19} \text{ c.}$$

$$95 \text{ " } \ldots \ldots \ldots 285 + 15 = 300 \text{ c.)}$$

If the teacher has faithfully followed this course, the pupils are prepared for a practical arithmetic, and they should be given a book having a great many examples methodically arranged. With such a book, they will be able to solve and explain the examples from beginning to end. The teacher must give a great many original examples. On the other hand, he must not feel bound to use all of the examples in this book with which to drill his pupils. He must use judgment and common sense in the application of the principles and methods herein given.

Not many kinds, but much, is the motto with which Grube closes his work on Number.

BOOKS FOR TEACHERS.

CLASSIFIED LIST UNDER SUBJECTS.

To aid purchasers to procure books best suited to their purpose, we give below a list of our publications under subjects. This division is sometimes a difficult one to make, so that we have in many cases placed the same book under several titles; for instance, Currie's Early Education appears under PRINCIPLES AND PRACTICE OF EDUCATION and also PRIMARY EDUCATION.

HISTORY OF EDUCATION.

	Retail,	Our Price to Teachers	By Mail Extra
Kellogg's Life of Pestalozzi, - - - - - - paper	.15	.12	.01
Rissehart's History of Education, - - - - - cl.	.25	.20	.03
Quick's Educational Reformers, - - - - - cl.	1.00	.80	.08
Browning's Educational Theories, - - - - cl.	.50	.40	.05

KINDERGARTEN EDUCATION.

Autobiography of Froebel, - - - - - cl.	.50	.40	.05
Hoffman's Kindergarten Gifts - - - - - paper	.16	.12	.01

METHODS OF TEACHING.

Calkins' Ear and Voice Training, - - - cl.	.50	.40	.05
Dewey's How to Teach Munners, - - - cl.	.50	.40	.05
Johnson's Education by Doing, - - - cl.	.75	.60	.05
Partridge's Quincy Methods, - - - - cl.	1.75	1.40	.13
Shaw and Donnell's School Devices,- - - cl.	1.25	1.00	.09
Seeley's Grube Method of Teaching Arithmetic, - cl.	1.00	.80	.07
Seeley's Grube Idea in Teaching Arithmetic, - cl.	.30	.24	.03
Woodhull's Easy Experiments in Science, - - cl.	.50	.40	.05
Gladstone's Object Teaching, - - - - paper	.15	.12	.01
McMurray's How to Conduct the Recitation,- -paper	.15	.12	.01

MANUAL TRAINING.

Love's Industrial Education, - - - - cl.	1.50	1.20	.12
Leland's Practical Education, - - - - cl.	2.00	1.60	.10
Butler's Argument for Manual Training, - - paper	.15	.12	.01

MISCELLANEOUS.

Blaikies on Self Cuture, - - - - - - cl-	.25	.20	.03
Gardner's Town and Country School Buildings, - cl.	2.50	2.00	.12
Wilhelm's Student's Calendar, - - - - paper	.30	.24	.03
Pooler's N. Y. School Law,- - - - - cl.	.30	.24	.03
Rissehart's System of Education, - - - cl.	.25	.20	.03
Lubbock's Best 100 Books, - - - - - paper	.20	.16	.02
Allen's Temperament in Education, - - - cL	.50	.40	.05
Fitch's Improvement in Education, - - - paper	.15	.12	.01
Augsburg's Easy Things to Draw, - - - paper	.30	.24	.03

PRINCIPLES AND PRACTICE OF EDUCATION.

Parker's Talks on Teaching, - - - - cl.	1.25	1.00	.00
" Practical Teacher, - - - - cl.	1.50	1.20	.14
Fitch's Lectures on Teaching, - - - - cl.	1.25	1.00	pd.
Currie's Early Education, - - - - - cl.	1.25	1 00	.08
Hughes' Mistakes in Teaching, - - - - cl.	.50	.40	.05
" Securing and Retaining Attention, - cl.	.50	.40	.05
Southwick's Quiz manual of Teaching - - - cl.	.75	.60	.00
Fitch's Art of Questioning, - - - - paper	.15	.12	.01
" " Securing Attention - - - paper	.15	.12	01
Quick's How to Train the Memory, - - - paper	.15	.12	.01
Yonge's Practical Work in School, - - - paper	.15	.12	.01

PSYCHOLOGY AND EDUCATION.

Welch's Teachers' Psychology, - - - - - cl.	1.25	1.00	.09
" Talks on Psychology, - - - - cl.	.50	.40	.05
Allen's Mind Studies for Young Teachers, - - cl.	.50	.40	.05
Perez's First Three Years of Childhood, - - - cl.	1.50	1.20	.10
Allen's Temperament in Education, - - - - cl.	.50	.40	.05

PRINCIPLES OF EDUCATION.

Rissehart's Principles of Eduation, - - - - cl.	.25	.20	.03
Payne's Lectures on Science and Art of Eduation, cl.	$1.00	.80	.07
Tate's Philosophy of Education, - - - - cl.	1.50	1.20	.09
Teachers' Manual Series - - - - each, paper	.15	.12	.01
Huntington's Unconscious Tuition, - - - -paper	.15	.12	.01
Carter's Artificial Stupidity in School, - - -paper	.15	.12	.01

PRIMARY EDUCATION.

Augsburg's Easy Things to Draw, - - - -paper	.30	.24	.03
Augsburg's Easy Drawings for Geog. Class, - - cl.	.50	.40	.05
Currie's Early Education, - - - - - - cl.	1.25	1.00	.08
Parker's Talks on Teaching, - - - - - cl.	1.25	1.00	.09
Partridge's Quincy Methods, - - - - - cl.	1.75	1.40	.13
Perez's First Three Years of Childhood, - - cl.	1.50	1.20	.01
Calkins' Ear and Voice Training - - - - cl.	.50	.40	.05
Gladstone's Object Teaching, - - - -paper	.15	.12	.01
Johnson's Education by Doing, - - - - cl.	.75	.60	.05
Seeley's Grube Method of Teaching Arithmetic, - cl.	1.00	.80	.07
Seeley's Grube Idea in Primary Arithmetic, - - cl.	.30	.32	.03

QUESTION BOOKS FOR TEACHERS.

Shaw's National Question Book, - - - -	1.75		pd.
N. Y. State Examination Questions, - - - cl.	1.00	.80	.08
Analytical Question Series. Geography, - - cl.	.50	.40	.05
" " " U. S. History Series, - cl.	.50	.40	.05
" " " Grammar, - - - cl.	.50	.40	.05
Southwick's Quiz Manual of the Theory and Practice of Teaching, - - - - - - - cl.	.75	.60	.0

SCHOOL MANAGEMENT.

Kellogg's School Management, - - - - - cl.	.75	.60	.05
Hughes' How to Keep Order, - - - - -paper	.15	.12	.01
Sidgwick's Stimulus in School, - - - - -paper	.15	.12	.01

SCHOOL HYGIENE.

Groff's School Hygiene, - - - - - -paper	.15	.12	.01

SCHOOL APPARATUS.

' Standard" Manikin. (Sold by subscription.)		
" Man Wonderful " Manikin, - - - - -	5.00	pd.
Standard Blackboard Stencils, 500 different nos., from 5 to 50 cents each. Send for special list.		
" Unique " Pencil Sharpener, - - - - -	1.50	.10
Standard Physician's Manikin. (Sold by subscription.)		

SINGING AND DIALOGUE BOOKS.

Southwick's Handy Helps, - - - - - - cl.	1.00	.80	.08
Song Treasures, - - - - - - - -paper	.15	.12	.02
Reception Day Series, (6 Nos.) - - - each, paper	.30	.24	.03

☞ 64-page descriptive catalogue of these books free to any address. Large 128-page descriptive catalogue of all best educational books published, with prices and special rates to teachers, 6 cents.

Payne's Lectures on the Science and

ART OF EDUCATION. *Reading Circle Edition.* By JOSEPH PAYNE, the first Professor of the Science and Art of Education in the College of Preceptors, London, England. With portrait. 16mo, 350 pp., English cloth, with gold back stamp. Price, $1.00 ; *to teachers,* 80 cents ; by mail, 7 cents extra. *Elegant new edition from new plates.*

JOSEPH PAYNE.

Teachers who are seeking to know the principles of education will find them clearly set forth in this volume. It must be remembered that principles are the basis upon which all methods of teaching must be founded. So valuable is this book that if a teacher were to decide to own but three works on education, this would be one of them. This edition contains all of Mr. Payne's writings that are in any other American abridged edition, and *is the only one with his portrait.* It is far superior to any other edition published.

WHY THIS EDITION IS THE BEST.

(1.) The *side-titles.* These give the contents of the page. (2.) The analysis of each lecture, with reference to the *educational* points in it. (3.) The general analysis pointing out the three great principles found at the beginning. (4.) The index, where, under such heads as Teaching, Education, The Child, the important utterances of Mr. Payne are set forth. (5.) Its handy shape, large type, fine paper, and press-work and tasteful binding. All of these features make this a most valuable book. To obtain all these features in one edition, it was found necessary to *get out this new edition.*

Ohio Educational Monthly.—"It does not deal with shadowy theories; it is intensely practical."

Philadelphia Educational News.—"Ought to be in library of every progressive teacher."

Educational Courant.—"To know how to teach, more is needed than a knowledge of the branches taught. This is especially valuable."

Pennsylvania Journal of Education.—"Will be of practical value to Normal Schools and Institute."

Welch's Teachers' Psychology.

A Treatise on the Intellectual Faculties, the Order of the Growth, and the Corresponding Series of Studies by which they are Educated. By the late A. S. Welch, Professor of Psychology, Iowa Agricultural College, formerly Pres. of the Mich. Normal School. Cloth, 12mo, 300 pp., $1.25; *to teachers*, $1; by mail, 12 cents extra. Special terms to Normal Schools and Reading Circles.

A mastery of the branches to be taught was once thought to be an all-sufficient preparation for teaching. But it is now seen that there must be a knowledge of the mind that is to be trained. Psychology is the foundation of intelligent pedagogy. Prof. Welch undertook to write a book that should deal with mind-unfolding, as exhibited in the school-room. He shows what is meant by attending, memorizing, judging, abstracting, imagining, classifying, etc., as it is done by the pupil over his text-books. First, there is the *concept;* then there is (1) gathering concepts, (2) storing concepts, (3) dividing concepts, (4) abstracting concepts, (5) building concepts, (6) grouping concepts, (7) connecting concepts, (8) deriving concepts. Each of these is clearly explained and illustrated; the reader instead of being bewildered over strange terms comprehends that imagination means a building up of concepts, and so of the other terms.

DR. A. S. WELCH.

A most valuable part of the book is its application to practical education. How to train these powers that deal with the concept—that is the question. There must be exercises to train the mind to *gather, store, divide, abstract, build, group, connect,* and *derive* concepts. The author shows what studies do this appropriately, and where there are mistakes made in the selection of studies. The book will prove a valuable one to the teacher who wishes to know the structure of the mind and the way to minister to its growth. It would seem that at last a psychology had been written that would be a real aid, instead of a hindrance, to clear knowledge.

Allen's Mind Studies for Young Teach-

ERS. By Jerome Allen, Ph.D., Associate Editor of the
School Journal, Prof. of Pedagogy, Univ. of City of
N. Y. 16mo, large, clear type, 128 pp.   Cloth, 50 cents ; *to
teachers*, 40 cents ; by mail, 5 cents extra.

JEROME ALLEN, Ph.D., Associate Editor
of the *Journal* and *Institute*.

There are many teachers who
know little about psychology,
and who desire to be better in-
formed concerning its principles, especially its relation to the
work of teaching. For the aid
of such, this book has been prepared. But it is not a psychology—only an introduction to it,
aiming to give some fundamental principles, together with
something concerning the phi-
losophy of education. Its method is subjective rather than ob-
jective, leading the student to
watch mental processes, and
draw his own conclusions. It
is written in language easy to
be comprehended, and has many
practical illustrations.   It will
aid the teacher in his daily work
in dealing with mental facts and states.

To most teachers psychology seems to be dry. This book shows
how it may become the most interesting of all studies. It also
shows how to begin the knowledge of self. " We cannot know
in others what we do not first know in ourselves." This is the
key-note of this book. Students of elementary psychology will
appreciate this feature of " Mind Studies."

ITS CONTENTS.

CHAP.
I. How to Study Mind.
II. Some Facts in Mind Growth.
III. Development.
IV. Mind Incentives.
V. A few Fundamental Principles Settled.
VI. Temperaments.
VII. Training of the Senses.
VIII. Attention.
IX. Perception.
X. Abstraction.
XI. Faculties used in Abstract Thinking.

CHAP.
XII. From the Subjective to the Conceptive.
XIII. The Will.
XIV. Diseases of the Will.
XV. Kinds of Memory.
XVI. The Sensibilities.
XVII. Relation of the Sensibilities to the Will.
XVIII. Training of the Sensibilities.
XIX. Relation of the Sensibilities to Morality.
XX. The Imagination.
XXI. Imagination in its Maturity.
XXII. Education of the Moral Sense.

Perez's First Three Years of Childhood.

AN EXHAUSTIVE STUDY OF THE PSYCHOLOGY OF CHILDREN. By BERNARD PEREZ. Edited and translated by ALICE M. CHRISTIE, translator of " Child and Child Nature," with an introduction by JAMES SULLY, M.A., author of " Outlines of Psychology," etc. 12mo, cloth, 324 pp. Price, $1.50 ; *to teachers,* $1.20 ; by mail, 10 cents extra.

This is a comprehensive treatise on the psychology of childhood, and is a practical study of the human mind, not full formed and equipped with knowledge, but as nearly as possible, *ab origine*—before habit, environment, and education have asserted their sway and made their permanent modifications. The writer looks into all the phases of child activity. He treats exhaustively, and in bright Gallic style, of sensations, instincts, sentiments, intellectual tendencies, the will, the faculties of æsthetic and moral senses of young children. He shows how ideas of truth and falsehood arise in little minds, how natural is imitation and how deep is credulity. He illustrates the development of imagination and the elaboration of new concepts through judgment, abstraction, reasoning, and other mental methods. It is a book that has been long wanted by all who are engaged in teaching, and especially by all who have to do with the education and training of children.

This edition has a new index of special value, and the book is carefully printed and elegantly and durably bound. Be sure to get our standard edition.

OUTLINE OF CONTENTS.

CHAP.
I. Faculties of Infant before Birth—First Impression of Newborn Child.
II. Motor Activity at the Beginning of Life—at Six Months——at Fifteen Months.
III. Instinctive and Emotional Sensations—First Perceptions.
IV. General and Special Instincts.
V. The Sentiments.
VI. Intellectual Tendencies—Veracity—Imitation—Credulity.
VII. The Will.
VIII. Faculties of Intellectual Acquisition and Retention—Attention—Memory.

CHAP.
IX. Association of Psychical States—Association—Imagination.
X. Elaboration of Ideas—Judgment — Abstraction — Comparison — Generalization — Reasoning—Errors and Allusions—Errors and Allusions Owing to Moral Causes.
XI. Expression and Language.
XII. Æsthetic Senses — Musical Sense — Sense of Material Beauty — Constructive Instinct—Dramatic Instinct.
XIII. Personalty — Reflection—Moral Sense.

Col. Francis W. Parker, Principal Cook County Normal and Training School, Chicago, says:—" I am glad to see that you have published Perez's wonderful work upon childhood. I shall do all I can to get everybody to read it. It is a grand work."

John Bascom, Pres. Univ. of Wisconsin, says:—" A work of marked interest."

G. Stanley Hall, Professor of Psychology and Pedagogy, Johns Hopkins Univ., says:—" I esteem the work a very valuable one for primary and kindergarten teachers, and for all interested in the psychology of childhood."

And many other strong commendations.

Parker's Talks on Teaching.

Notes of "Talks on Teaching" given by COL. FRANCIS W. PARKER (formerly Superintendent of schools of Quincy, Mass.), before the Martha's Vineyard Institute, Summer of 1882. Reported by LELIA E. PATRIDGE. Square 16mo, 5x6 1-2 inches, 192 pp., *laid* paper, English cloth. Price, $1.25 ; *to teachers*, $1.00 ; by mail, 9 cents extra.

The methods of teaching employed in the schools of Quincy, Mass., were seen to be the methods of nature. As they were copied and explained, they awoke a great desire on the part of those who could not visit the schools to know the underlying principles. In other words, Colonel Parker was asked to explain *why* he had his teachers teach thus. In the summer of 1882, in response to requests, Colonel Parker gave a course of lectures before the Martha's Vineyard Institute, and these were reported by Miss Patridge, and published in this book.

The book became famous ; more copies were sold of it in the same time than of any other educational book whatever. The daily papers, which usually pass by such books with a mere mention, devoted columns to reviews of it.

The following points will show why the teacher will want this book.

1. It explains the "New Methods." There is a wide gulf between the new and the old education. Even school boards understand this.

2. It gives the underlying principles of education. For it must be remembered that Col. Parker is not expounding *his* methods, but the methods of nature.

3. It gives the ideas of a man who is evidently an "educational genius," a man born to understand and expound education. We have few such ; they are worth everything to the human race.

4. It gives a biography of Col. Parker. This will help the teacher of education to comprehend the man and his motives.

5. It has been adopted by nearly every State Reading Circle.

Hughes' Mistakes in Teaching.

By JAMES J. HUGHES, Inspector of Schools, Toronto, Canada. Cloth, 16mo, 115 pp. Price, 50 cents; *to teachers*, 40 cents; by mail, 5 cents extra.

JAMES L. HUGHES, Inspector of Schools, Toronto, Canada.

Thousands of copies of the old edition have been sold. The new edition is worth double the old; the material has been increased, restated, and greatly improved. Two new and important Chapters have been added on "Mistakes in Aims," and "Mistakes in Moral Training." Mr. Hughes says in his preface: "In issuing a revised edition of this book, it seems fitting to acknowledge gratefully the hearty appreciation that has been accorded it by American teachers. Realizing as I do that its very large sale indicates that it has been of service to many of my fellow-teachers, I have recognized the duty of enlarging and revising it so as to make it still more helpful in preventing the common mistakes in teaching and training."

This is one of the six books recommended by the N. Y. State Department to teachers preparing for examination for State certificates.

CAUTION.

Our new AUTHORIZED COPYRIGHT EDITION, *entirely rewritten by the author, is the only one to buy. It is beautifully printed and handsomely bound. Get no other.*

CONTENTS OF OUR NEW EDITION.

CHAP. I. 7 Mistakes in Aim.

CHAP. II. 21 Mistakes in School Management.

CHAP. III. 24 Mistakes in Discipline.

CHAP. IV. 27 Mistakes in Method.

CHAP. V. 13 Mistakes in Moral Training.

☞ *Chaps. I. and V. are entirely new.*

Hughes' Securing and Retaining Atten-

TION. By JAMES L. HUGHES, Inspector Schools, Toronto, Canada, author of "Mistakes in Teaching." Cloth, 116 pp. Price, 50 cents; *to teachers*, 40 cents; by mail, 5 cents extra.

This valuable little book has already become widely known to American teachers. Our new edition has been almost *entirely re-written*, and several new important chapters added. It is the only AUTHORIZED COPYRIGHT EDITION. *Caution.*—Buy no other.

WHAT IT CONTAINS.

I. General Principles; II. Kinds of Attention; III. Characteristics of Good Attention; IV. Conditions of Attention; V. Essential Characteristics of the Teacher in Securing and Retaining Attention; VI. How to Control a Class; VII. Methods of Stimulating and Controlling a Desire for Knowledge; VIII. How to Gratify and Develop the Desire for Mental Activity; IX. Distracting Attention; X. Training the Power of Attention; XI. General Suggestions regarding Attention.

TESTIMONIALS.

S. P. Robbins, Pres. McGill Normal School, Montreal, Can., writes to Mr. Hughes:—"It is quite superfluous for me to say that your little books are admirable. I was yesterday authorized to put the 'Attention' on the list of books to be used in the Normal School next year. Crisp and attractive in style, and mighty by reason of its good, sound common-sense, it is a book that every teacher should know."

Popular Educator (Boston):—"Mr. Hughes has embodied the best thinking of his life in these pages."

Central School Journal (Ia.).—"Though published four or five years since, this book has steadily advanced in popularity."

Educational Courant (Ky.).—"It is intensely practical. There isn't a mystical, muddy expression in the book."

Educational Times (England).—"On an important subject, and admirably executed."

School Guardian (England).—"We unhesitatingly recommend it."

New England Journal of Education.—"The book is a guide and a manual of special value."

New York School Journal.—"Every teacher would derive benefit from reading this volume."

Chicago Educational Weekly.—"The teacher who aims at best success should study it."

Phil. Teacher.—"Many who have spent months in the school-room would be benefited by it."

Maryland School Journal.—"Always clear, never tedious."
Va. Ed. Journal.—"Excellent hints as to securing attention."
Ohio Educational Monthly.—"We advise readers to send for a copy."
Pacific Home and School Journal.—"An excellent little manual."
Prest. James H. Hoose, State Normal School, Cortland, N. Y., says:— "The book must prove of great benefit to the profession."
Supt. A. W. Edson, Jersey City, N. J., says:—"A good treatise has long been needed, and Mr. Hughes has supplied the want."

Calkins' Ear and Voice Training by

MEANS OF ELEMENTARY SOUNDS OF LANGUAGE. By N. A. CALKINS, Assistant Superintendent N. Y. City Schools; author of "Primary Object Lessons," "Manual of Object Teaching," "Phonic Charts," etc. Cloth. 16mo, about 100 pp. Price, 50 cents; *to teachers*, 40 cents; by mail, 5 cents extra.

An idea of the character of this work may be had by the following extracts from its *Preface:*

" The common existence of abnormal sense perception among school children is a serious obstacle in teaching. This condition is most

obvious in the defective perceptions of sounds and forms. It may be seen in the faulty articulations in speaking and reading; in the inability to distinguish musical sounds readily; also in the common mistakes made in hearing what is said. . . .

" Careful observation and long experience lead to the conclusion that the most common defects in sound perceptions exist because of lack of proper training in childhood to develop this power of the mind into activity through the sense of hearing. It becomes, therefore, a matter of great importance in education, that in the training of children due attention shall be given to the development of ready and accurate perceptions of sounds.

" How to give this training so as to secure the desired results is a subject that deserves the careful attention of parents and teachers.

SUPT. N. A. CALKINS.

Much depends upon the manner of presenting the sounds of our language to pupils, whether or not the results shall be the development in sound-perceptions that will *train the ear and voice* to habits of distinctness and accuracy in speaking and reading.

" The methods of teaching given in this book are the results of an extended experience under such varied conditions as may be found with pupils representing all nationalities, both of native and foreign born children. The plans described will enable teachers to lead their pupils to acquire ready and distinct perceptions through sense training, and cause them to know the sounds of our language in a manner that will give practical aid in learning both the spoken and the written language. The simplicity and usefulness of the lessons need only to be known to be appreciated and used."

Dewey's How to Teach Manners in the

SCHOOL-ROOM. By Mrs. JULIA M. DEWEY, Principal of the Normal School at Lowell, Mass., formerly Supt. of Schools at Hoosick Falls, N. Y. Cloth, 16mo, 104 pp. Price, **50** cents; *to teachers*, 40 cents; by mail, 5 cents extra.

Many teachers consider the manners of a pupil of little importance so long as he is industrious. But the boys and girls are to be fathers and mothers; **some** of the boys will stand in places of importance as professional men, and they will carry the mark of ill-breeding all their lives. Manners **can** be taught in the school-room: they render the school-room **more** attractive; they banish tendencies to misbehavior. In this volume Mrs. Dewey has shown how manners can be taught. The method is to present some fact of deportment, and then lead the children to discuss its bearings; thus they learn why good manners are to be learned and practised. The printing and binding are exceedingly neat and attractive."

OUTLINE OF CONTENTS.

Introduction.
General Directions.
Special Directions to Teachers.

LESSONS ON MANNERS FOR YOUNGEST PUPILS.

Lessons on **Manners — Second** Two Years.
Manners in School—First Two Years.
"   "   Second   "
Manners at Home—First   "
"   "   Second   "
Manners in Public—First   "
"   "   Second   "

Table Manners—First Two Years.
"   "   Second   "

LESSONS ON MANNERS FOR ADVANCED PUPILS.
Manners in School.
Personal Habits.
Manners in Public.
Table Manners.
Manners in Society.
Miscellaneous Items.
Practical Training in Manners.
Suggestive Stories, Fables, Anecdotes, and Poems.
Memory Gems.

Central School Journal.—"It furnishes illustrative lessons."

Texas School Journal.—"They (the pupils) will **carry** the mark of ill-breeding all their lives (unless taught otherwise)."

Pacific Ed. Journal.—"Principles are **enforced by anecdote and conversation.**"

Teacher's Exponent.—"We believe such a book **will** be very welcome."

National Educator.—"Common-sense suggestions."

Ohio Ed. Monthly.—"Teachers would do well to get it."

Nebraska Teacher.—"Many teachers consider manners of little importance, but some of the boys will stand in places of importance."

School Educator.—"The spirit of the author is commendable."

School Herald.—"These lessons are full of suggestions."

Va. School Journal.—"Lessons furnished in a delightful style."

Miss. Teacher.—"The best presentation we have seen."

Ed. Courant.—"It is simple, straightforward, and plain."

Iowa Normal Monthly,—"Practical and well-arranged lessons on manners."

Progressive Educator.—"Will prove to be **most** helpful to the teacher who desires her pupils to be well-mannered."

Patridge's "Quincy Methods."

The "Quincy Methods," illustrated; Pen photographs from the Quincy schools. By LELIA E. PATRIDGE. Illustrated with a number of engravings, and two colored plates. Blue cloth, gilt, 12mo, 686 pp.   Price, $1.75; *to teachers*, $1.40; by mail, 13 cents extra.

When the schools of Quincy, Mass., became so famous under the superintendence of Col. Francis W. Parker, thousands of teachers visited them. Quincy became a sort of "educational Mecca," to the disgust of the routinists, whose schools were passed by. Those who went to study the methods pursued there were called on to tell what they had seen. Miss Patridge was one of those who visited the schools of Quincy; in the Pennsylvania Institutes (many of which she conducted), she found the teachers were never tired of being told how things were done in Quincy. She revisited the schools several times, and wrote down what she saw; then the book was made.

1. This book presents the actual practice in the schools of Quincy. It is composed of "pen photographs."

2. It gives abundant reasons for the great stir produced by the two words "Quincy Methods." There are reasons for the discussion that has been going on among the teachers of late years.

3. It gives an insight to principles underlying real education as distinguished from book learning.

4. It shows the teacher not only what to do, but gives the way in which to do it.

5. It impresses one with the *spirit* of the Quincy schools.

6. It shows the teacher how to create an *atmosphere* of happiness, of busy work, and of progress.

7. It shows the teacher how not to waste her time in worrying over disorder.

8. It tells how to treat pupils with courtesy, and get courtesy back again.

9. It presents four years of work, considering Number, Color, Direction, Dimension, Botany, Minerals, Form, Language, Writing, Pictures, Modelling, Drawing, Singing, Geography, Zoology, etc., etc.

10. There are 686 pages; a large book devoted to the realities of school life, in realistic descriptive language. It is plain, real, not abstruse and uninteresting.

11. It gives an insight into real education, the education urged by Pestalozzi, Frœbel, Mann, Page, Parker, etc.

Shaw and Donnell's School Devices.

"SCHOOL DEVICES." A book of ways and suggestions for teachers. By EDWARD R. SHAW and WEBB DONNELL, of the High School at Yonkers, N. Y. Illustrated. Dark-blue cloth binding, gold, 16mo, 289 pp. Price, $1.25; *to teachers*, $1.00; by mail, 9 cents extra.

This valuable book has just been greatly improved by the addition of nearly 75 pages of entirely new material.

☞A BOOK OF "WAYS" FOR TEACHERS.☜

Teaching is an art; there are "ways to do it." This book is made to point out "ways," and to help by suggestions.

1. It gives "ways" for teaching Language, Grammar, Reading, Spelling, Geography, etc. These are in many cases novel; they are designed to help attract the attention of the pupil.

2. The "ways" given are not the questionable "ways" so often seen practised in school-rooms, but are in accord with the spirit of modern educational ideas.

3. This book will afford practical assistance to teachers who wish to keep their work from degenerating into mere routine. It gives them, in convenient form for constant use at the desk, a multitude of new ways in which to present old truths. The great enemy of the teacher is want of interest. Their methods do not attract attention. There is no teaching unless there is *attention*. The teacher is too apt to think there is but one "way" of teaching spelling; he thus falls into a rut. Now there are many "ways" of teaching spelling, and some "ways" are better than others. Variety must exist in the school-room; the authors of this volume deserve the thanks of the teachers for pointing out methods of obtaining variety without sacrificing the great end sought—scholarship. New "ways" induce greater effort, and renewal of activity.

4. The book gives the result of large actual experience in the school-room, and will meet the needs of thousands of teachers, by placing at their command that for which visits to other schools are made, institutes and associations attended, viz., new ideas and fresh and forceful ways of teaching. The devices given under Drawing and Physiology are of an eminently practical nature, and cannot fail to invest these subjects with new interest. The attempt has been made to present only devices of a practical character.

5. The book suggests "ways" to make teaching *effective;* it is not simply a book of new "ways," but of "ways" that will produce good results.

Woodhull's Simple Experiments for the

School-Room. By Prof. John F. Woodhull, Prof. of Natural Science in the College for the Training of Teachers, New York City, author of "Manual of Home-Made Apparatus." Cloth, 16mo. Price, 50 cents; *to teachers,* 40 cents; by mail, 5 cents extra.

This book contains a series of simple, easily-made experiments, to perform which will aid the comprehension of every-day phenomena. They are really the very lessons given by the author in the Primary and Grammar Departments of the Model School in the College for the Training of Teachers, New York City.

The apparatus needed for the experiments consists, for the most part, of such things as every teacher will find at hand in a school-room or kitchen. The experiments are so connected in logical order as to form a continuous exhibition of the phenomena of *combustion. This book is not a science catechism.* Its aim is to train the child's mind in habits of reasoning by experimental methods.

These experiments should be made in every school of our country, and thus bring in a scientific method of dealing with nature. The present method of cramming children's minds with isolated facts of which they can have no adequate comprehension is a ruinous and unprofitable one. This book points out the method employed by the *best teachers in the best schools.*

WHAT IT CONTAINS.

I. Experiments with Paper.	VI. Air as an Agent in Combustion.
II. " " Wood.	VII. Products of Complete "
III. " " a Candle.	VIII. Currents of Air, etc.—Ventila-
IV. " " Kerosene.	IX. Oxygen of the Air. [tion.
V. Kindling Temperature.	X. Chemical Changes.

In all there are 91 experiments described, illustrated by 35 engravings.

Jas. H. Canfield, Univ. of Kans., Lawrence, says:—"I desire to say most emphatically that the method pursued is the only true one in all school work. Its spirit is admirable. We need and must have far more of this instruction."

J. C. Packard, Univ. of Iowa, Iowa City, says:—"For many years shut up to the simplest forms of illustrative apparatus, I learned that the necessity was a blessing, since so much could be accomplished by home-made apparatus—inexpensive and effective."

Henry R. Russell, Woodbury, N. J., Supt. of the Friends School:—"Admirable little book. It is just the kind of book we need."

S. T. Dutton, Supt. Schools, New Haven, Ct.—"Contains just the kind of help teachers need in adapting natural science to common schools."